The Hidden History of Australia

by

Bill Hornadge

Watsons Bay, Sydney

An **IMPRINT** book

Imprint is a division of ETT Imprint
11 Cove Street, Watsons Bay, NSW 2030, Australia

First published in 1997 by ETT Imprint

ISBN 1 875892 59 1

Prestidigitation by Mike Connolly
Printed in Australia by McPhersons Printing Group

Contents

Preface

Scattered across Australia are mini-mountains of the tailings of countless abandoned mines - gold, silver and other valuable ores, the only relics of the great mining booms of the 19th Century. These discarded tailings are known as mullock heaps and they still seem a happy hunting ground for modern fossickers looking for that elusive glint of gold, silver or opal. And some do make occasional "finds" - even if they seem to be mighty reluctant to share the story of their success with the Taxation Department!

If I were more energetic I would probably join them in this never-ending guest for the Earth's rich bounty, but being a sedentary type I prefer to do my fossicking in the mullock heaps of history, always hoping for a find or two that the professionals who have mined before me may have missed.

And it is surprising how much history there is yet to be unearthed. Although we are a comparatively young country, there are huge gaps in the story of this vast land since 1788, and before that, our knowledge is pitifully small in the historic sense.

The professional historians are not really to blame for this state of affairs. None existed in the first half of the last century and thus we have to rely almost entirely on old diaries and family papers, supplemented by unsatisfactory official records. In the latter half of the last century, and early part of this century, the numbers of professional historians were few, their remuneration pitiful and their research funds virtually zero. Many survived only by churning out juvenile textbooks for the schools and to do this were forced to fall back on those old standbyes of historians through the ages - explorers, politics, "famous people" and so-called Great Events. And the latter were thin on the ground as we had no serious revolutions and went off to war in faraway places.

There were whole areas in which our historians were not tempted to explore through lack of interest or other pressures. Among these virtually untapped fields were those of commerce and industry even though these activities affected the daily lives of most Australians more than an army of explorers could ever do.

And where are these mullock heaps of history I speak about? In family diaries and papers, local town records, museums and libraries, in old newspapers and magazines, in books that appeared briefly on the market and which have long been out of print and inaccessible to most researchers. The list is endless. The material is there in abundance. .

In this volume I present a selection of these stories about people, places and events which I have gathered over several decades of dedicated fossicking. I believe that what every student of history should be doing is to be continually crying why? Why this? Why that? Why the other? More especially we should be going around in our daily lives asking of those who control our destinies questions which they would prefer not to answer on the grounds that they might expose their inadequacies or misdeeds.

Asking awkward questions in former ages was of course a pretty dangerous business and one could easily lose an arm, a leg or a head by asking the WRONG question at the wrong time. These are more tolerant times, though more than one whistleblower has come to grief in more recent times as I have demonstrated in several of the stories presented in this volume.

Bill Hornadge

1

The Boat People

Boat people from Up North have been pouring into the Sunburnt Country in increasing numbers of late to the great consternation of some citizens. So, what's new?

Boat People have been arriving on our shores on a pretty regular basis for at the very least 40,000 years (some archaeologists now believe this time span may be pushed back well beyond 100,000 years but concrete evidence for this theory is still lacking).

Back in January 1788 a whole fleet of these undesirables arrived at a place called Botany Bay and caused no end of trouble for the older, long-established settlers of the place.

Just how many of these dark-skinned settlers were around in 1788 has always been a matter of dispute. Early guesses, based on reports of sundry inland explorers and pioneer settlers, put the overall figure for the continent at around 300,000. But more recent archaeological discoveries, particularly in the Murray-Darling river basins, have forced scientists to sharply revise this figure upwards. What is not in great dispute is the fact that the bulk of the aboriginal population were located in the then fertile inland areas of the continent, not clustered around the coast as is the practice of the latter-day white settlers. And the early white-skinned settlers can thank their lucky stars that this was so, otherwise they might well have suffered the fate of so many other pioneering settlements around the world - in the Caribbean for example - who were wiped out by hostile indigenes.

When Captain Phillip and his small fleet arrived at Botany Bay, and later Sydney Cove, in 1788 to take possession of this vast continent we now call Australia, he encountered no initial resistance from the relatively small scattered groups of the Eora people located around the Sydney waterways extending to the Hawkesbury River in the north, to the Georges River in the south and inland to the foothills of the Blue Mountains, an overall area of approximately 1800 square kilometres.

In this large area were numerous small sub-groups of the Eora people - more like extended family groups than formalised tribes - all speaking closely related languages and dialects. Since food was relatively plentiful, the groups lived in harmony. The Eora people were hunters and gatherers, not warriors. Nor were they united into great tribal nations like the Apache, the Sioux or the Mohicans of inland North America. In short, they were in no position to offer any serious resistance to these strange white people who arrived in huge canoes, adorned their bodies with garments and who carried dangerous spears which emitted fire and lumps of rock from their pointy-ends.

In the beginning these strangers did not exhibit any great hostility as Governor Phillip had received strict instructions to befriend the natives and to adopt conciliatory policies when dealing with them. Indeed the initial contacts where without much drama.

The first real contact came when the First Fleeters managed to capture a native named Arabanu. Initially he was tied up by the leg until he indicated he was willing to stay and learn the language and customs of the "whitey". As an early account says, he became one of the Governor's family. But, alas, this initial experiment in multiculturalism came to an abrupt end in May 1789 when the unlucky Arabanu died of smallpox. Score one point for white civilisation.

Not deterred by this minor setback the First Fleeters immediately went out and captured another native, Bennelong, who proved to be made of sterner stuff than Arabanu because he even scored (and survived) a trip to England where he was paraded around as an object of much curiosity.

But all this happy fraternising received a huge setback on December 9, 1790 when Governor Phillip's gamekeeper, a convict named John McIntyre, was speared in the arm by a native named Pemulway. And this was no small flesh wound as it was inflicted by a spear armed with jagged pieces of shell held in place by natural resin. The wound itself was seven inches long and was to prove fatal, though McIntyre clung to life for several weeks.

Initially he told his rescuers that the attack by Pemulway had been unprovoked but on his deathbed he confessed that it had been the result of a dispute over a native woman.

Governor Phillip was unaware of the circumstances behind the attack on his gamekeeper and over-reacted in a way that was out of character and in breach of explicit orders he had for the treatment of natives.

On December 13 he issued a General Order which was quite explicit in its intent: "Several tribes of the natives still continuing to throw their spears at any man they meet unarmed, by which several have been killed or dangerously wounded, the Governor, in order to deter the natives from such practices in future, has ordered out a party to search for the man who wounded the convict

(McIntyre) and to make a severe example of that tribe". In a latter part of the order Phillip instructed his force to capture six adult males, any six, so long as they were natives who resided near the head of Botany Bay. (Pemulway's natural hunting ground was in the western districts around where Penrith is now located, but at that time his tribe must have been on walkabout well to the east).

The order was considered so unusual, that it caused considerable dissent among the officers. Lieutenant Dawes considered it so unjust that he refused in writing to accompany the expedition, though he was later persuaded to go by the Chaplain, the Reverend Johnson. Captain Watkin Tench, who was ordered to lead the expedition, had similar reservations after the Governor ordered him to kill ten natives and bring their heads back to the settlement in sacks, and to take two prisoners who were to be brought back and executed in Sydney "in the most public and exemplary manner in the presence of as many of their countrymen as can be collected". Tench records that he persuaded the Governor to amend this order to reduce the number to six natives to be captured or shot.

The force that Captain Tench led out of Sydney on the morning of December 14 was a considerable one comprising two captains, two subalterns, three sergeants, two corporals, two surgeons, a drummer and forty privates.

Captain Tench's account of the expedition is instructive. He marched his force out with provisions for three days and with sufficient ropes to bind the expected prisoners and with hatchets to decapitate them and bags to hold the prize heads. The expedition set out at 4am and by nine o'clock had reached the peninsula at the head of Botany Bay. They continued to walk in various directions until four o'clock in the afternoon without sighting a single native.

They recommenced their search for the elusive Pemulway and

his tribe at dawn the next day but only succeeded in getting lost due to their guide having taken the wrong turning. However, during the morning they did sight five natives on a beach, but these wisely took to their heels and disappeared into the surrounding bush. They then proceeded to a small settlement of five small huts, only to see the few inhabitants of the place disappearing into the distance in three canoes.

But all was not lost that day. Later they did come across a single native fishing in shallow water. This native turned out to be friend, not foe, an aborigine named Colbee who was well-known around Sydney town. When Captain Tench questioned him about Pemulway, he fully understood the nature of their mission and said that Pemulway had fled to the south.

At that point Captain Tench seems to have realised the impossibility of his task. He made camp near a fresh water swamp and after restless night being invaded by swarms of mosquitoes and sandflies the weary troops trudged back to Sydney Town the next day without a single prisoner or head in a bag. Governor Phillip appears to have been extremely upset by the failure of the expedition because he ordered Captain Tench to take his troops out again.

The second expedition departed on December 22 and almost expired while crossing a creek near Botany Bay when most of the force became stuck in thick tenacious mud up to their waists. They were only saved from being sucked under this unfriendly goo when the few remaining soldiers who had not entered the stream quickly cut down some branches from nearby trees and managed to haul the stranded troops out of the mud. Even this strategy was not enough to save the sergeant of grenadiers who was so firmly stuck in the mud up to his breast bone that all preliminary efforts to get him out failed. He was finally saved when they managed to get some ropes intended for tying up native prisoners to him for fastening under his armpits.

After his troops had rested and cleaned the mud off their clothes, bodies and weapons, the force found a different less hostile crossing and made a quick advance towards a known native settlement, which Captain Tench planned to surround and raid at dawn the next day. He divided his troops into three units, each of whom was instructed to advance on the settlement from a different direction to arrive simultaneously. This manoeuvre was carried out with military precision, but to Captain Tench's surprise there was not a single native to be found, or a canoe to be sighted on the bay! The expedition spent the whole day in further searches without sighting any aborigines so Tench returned the following day to Sydney Town.

Governor Phillip seems to have accepted the fact that sending such forces out to capture Pemulway was a waste of time and energy. However, in the years to come he, and the settlers around Sydney Town were to hear much more of Pemulway. Little was known of Pemulway at the time despite the fact that before the spearing of McIntyre he had been in regular contact with the settlers. At the time of the attack it was estimated that that he was about thirty years of age, a very tall figure with a caste in one eye.

From the date of the two expeditions, Pemulway waged war on the white invaders, a war that lasted 12 years, and was the only long-term aboriginal resistance to be recorded in white settlement history.

In the first four years of this "undeclared war" an estimated twenty six whites were killed and thirteen wounded in various clashes with Pemulway's groups. The number of natives killed in the counter attacks by Government punitive expeditions or by settlers is not known, but must have been considerable. For much of the period of the "war" Pemelway had the assistance of an escaped convict, who was armed, and who would have been able to provide him with invaluable information about the movements and mentality of the government forces. Despite the fact that he had access to arms through soldiers and settlers killed in this war, Pemulway always kept to his traditional weapons of spears.

After the armed clashes of the early years of this war Pemulway must have realised he could not successfully pit spears against guns, even the crude weaponry of the 18th Century, so he changed his tactics to those of guerilla operations against the settlers around the western fringe of the colony. His favourite tactic was to wait until a crop was nearly ripe and almost ready for harvest, and then go in with his men in the dead of night with torches and attempt to burn it. Outlying shepherds huts and on occasion even homes of hostile settlers were also torched.

It was a very successful campaign which caused enormous problems for the early governors, and which only ended in 1802 when Pemulway was finally killed in an ambush. As Governor Phillip had directed twelve years earlier, his head was severed and carried to the then Governor Philip King, who had it preserved in a jar of spirits and sent off to England in the good ship Speedy. In a note he penned at the time to his friend Sir Joseph Banks, King wrote: "Although a Terrible Pest to the Colony, he was a brave and independent character".

When it arrived in England the severed head of Pemulway was put on display in the London Museum. In recent years approaches have been made to the British Government to have the head returned to Australia for proper burial, but the Museum has had to confess that this cannot be done because over the years this gruesome relic of the only real "war" between Australian aborigines and the white invaders has been "lost".

The Pemulway story inevitably invites speculation. What if things had been different when the Fleet first sailed into Botany Bay in 1788? What if the aborigines had been far more numerous on the coastal areas, instead of being grouped in their tens of thousands inland? And what if they had been grouped into organised warlike nations like the American Indians, with the Sydney tribe led by Pemulway?

For starters, the First Fleeters would have been so heavily outnumbered that Pemulway would have had no difficulty repelling any attempt to land the convicts, denying their application for Refugee Status (the application being rejected on the grounds of lack of personal hygiene on the part of the new arrivals), telling them bluntly to get knotted and rack off back home to whatever strange place they had come from. Interesting thought isn't it?

And what would have been the official reaction back in Whitehall when Phillip docked his fleet at Portsmouth with his even more bedraggled original cargo?

Would make a great movie or TV mini series, wouldn't it? We can just envisage the major set scene now as charismatic King Pemulway (brilliantly played by Ernie Dingo) gathers his forces at Kurnell and urges them on: "We've got them outnumbered ten to one. Come on, let's go for it!"

And on the deck of the Sirius stands the born-loser Captain Arthur Phillip (played by Laurie Brereton, now carving out a new career in the movies and, in this film symbolically back on his old turf of Botany Bay), ordering his usual set-piece retreat while blaming all about him for this new debacle. Exit fleet sailing over the horizon. Great stuff. Terrific drama. Where do I send the script?

2

Hiccups of History

One thing clearly stands out from any study of what happened in Australia in the early years after the white invasion (or settlement, if that terminology makes you feel more comfortable), and that is how *slow* things moved for a long time after 1788.

It took the new arrivals a quarter of a century to find their way across the Blue Mountains from Sydney Town; and it took them another quarter of a century to push settlement out to the western plains to where my home town of Dubbo stands today. And even then, half a century after white possession, it was not at all unusual for settlers out west to take four months or more to make the round trip by bullock wagon to the coast (usually to Morpeth) to take produce to market and return with provisions and other necessities for survival in the bush.

There were periods when time seemed to stand still, or inch forward at a snail's pace, broken only by some unforeseen event, or some unusual activity by an individual that sent a community edging off in a new direction. I call these incidents Hiccups of History and would like to illustrate three of them involving Dubbo, incidents which could be duplicated by communities all over the settled areas of the continent.

Dubbo was actually founded on its present location by just such a Hiccup of History when a young Frenchman had a near-fatal attack of appendicitis.

The Frenchman was Jean Emile de Bouillon Serisier, who was born in Bordeaux in 1824, the youngest son of Louis Alexandre de Bouillon Serisier, who in turn was the only surviving son of Jean Emile Count de Bouillon who along with his wife, daughter and another son had been executed in the reign of terror which followed the French revolution of 1789. Jean Emile's father had escaped the slaughter, and had fled to Bordeaux where he had built up a successful shipping and trading empire.

In 1840, at the age of 16, young Jean Emile went to Cuba to attend the wedding of his sister. He stayed on in Cuba for three years familiarising himself with his family trading interests.

In 1843 he decided to return to France on one of his father's ships then on an around the world trip via Cape Horn. Shortly before the ship reached Sydney he was stricken with severe appendicitis and had to be put ashore, with little chance of recovery as his condition was critical, and the ship sailed on without him. But young Serisier's constitution must have been strong as he did recover and was taken into the employ of his father's Sydney agents, Fesq & Despointes.

He proved a quick learner and when the firm decided to extend its operations into the western districts, they sent Jean Emile out to establish a trading post at Wellington - then the most westerly settlement in the colony. He was accompanied by a friend, Nicholas Hyeronimus, a young Belgian trader, also keen to develop trade in the west.

Serisier established a trading depot at Wellington, but quickly came to the conclusion that the real action was taking place further downstream on the Macquarie River as a result of a burgeoning overland traffic in cattle, which were being driven from the northern districts of the state to the lucrative southern markets of the relatively newly established town of Melbourne. These herds were making their crossing of the Macquarie River about thirty miles downstream from Wellington, near a squatter's run named "Dubbo" which had been established by Robert Dulhunty.

Accompanied by Hyeronimus, young Serisier travelled down to Old Dubbo Station with the idea of persuading Dulhunty to allow him to set up a trading depot to service the north-south overlanders and also a growing number of smaller "runs" west of the river.

Dulhunty saw the whole idea as an attempt to undermine his own trading activities and, after a violent quarrel, ordered both Serisier and Hyeronimus off his property. The pair travelled another six miles down-stream to the present day site of Dubbo where they made a deal with a more amenable small squatter named Dusty Bob.

On his land Serisier erected a small slab trading store and next to it Hyeronimus erected a crude slab building for an inn, the first Macquarie Inn. Apart from a couple of shepherds' huts, the only other buildings in the vicinity were a slab Court House and a slab Police Residence, both of which had been erected earlier that year (1847) at a cost of seventy five pounds for each building! The Dubbo settlement now comprised four law or commercial buildings but was without a name.

Serisier and Hyeronimus were also in a precarious situation, having no legal land tenure and having incurred the hostility of Dulhunty, the local magistrate and the district's largest land holder. To overcome this problem young Serisier organised a petition signed by all the small land holders of the district calling on the government to proclaim a village settlement. This the government did on August 28 1849, despite the strong opposition of Dulhunty and a rather derogatory finding by the surveyor appointed to lay out the village that "...the position of the village so near Wellington is not likely to make it a place of importance."

The surveyor was wrong and Serisier was right in his judgment about the site. Being a place of natural crossroads, Dubbo grew throughout the remainder of the century to become a major centre of the western districts. Its growth was in no small measure due to the energies of Jean Emile who played a leading role in almost every town organisation. He also prospered along with the town. He built two additional large general stores, while outside the town he had a showpiece estate 'Emulga', planted with 50,000 vines and with extensive cellars which in one bountiful year held 11,000 gallons of wine, making Dubbo one of the state's leading wine producing areas.

In 1859 Serisier married an English woman, Margaret Humphreys, and the couple had nine children. The eighth child, Daisy Marie Consolation, at the age of 17 married Count Charles de Wrobleski, a Polish nobleman then living in Sydney, and the following year persuaded him to start a newspaper, "Le Courrier Australien", to give a voice to French residents of Australia.

In 1879 Serisier decided to pay a long overdue visit to his native France, but on the voyage he contracted smallpox and died in Paris, on February 10 1880, aged 56. In today's terms it was a short life but one crammed with incident and achievement and tremendous contributions to his adopted land - all because of an attack of appendicitis.

The second example of a Dubbo based Hiccup of History occurred in 1877 while Serisier was still alive, and involved Josiah

Alfred Goode, who was born in London in 1821 and came to Australia at the age of 14. How he came to Dubbo is not recorded, but in 1856 he was a drover in the area on a weekly wage of a pound a week and with a drinking problem, when he met and married a 22-year-old widow, Mrs Mary Ann Bruce (described as being "in comfortable circumstances"). She was later to testify that at the time of the marriage she had three hundred pounds in the bank, cattle valued at one hundred and fifty pounds, and a considerable quantity of furniture and other assets.

Goode started a carrying business, using his wife's capital, while his wife ran a dairy and raised cattle, on a small property on the outskirts of the town. These joint ventures flourished to such an extent that two decades down the track Goode was a comparatively wealthy man, owning the farm, considerable land and cottages and the Exchange Hotel and adjoining shops. By that time he was an Alderman of the Dubbo Council and had overcome his drinking problem by signing the pledge of abstinence and was the founder and chairman of the local Temperance Lodge.

All this changed almost overnight in 1877 when the Holloway Company, a group of musical and theatrical performers, came to town. With the troupe was a 55-year-old actress and singer known as Madame Rowland (or Rolland or Rolande - accounts differ) who was destined to play the role of serpent in this western Garden of Eden.

Madame Rowland was born Eveline Rebecca Pierce, in Melbourne, in 1822. After leaving school she became a teacher and at one time was a schoolmistress at Richmond, in Victoria. She married a well-known Sydney musician named Samuel Bridges, and with him performed in concerts using the stage name of Madame Rowland in its various spellings. By the time she reached Dubbo with the Holloway Company, Bridges had disappeared from the scene. Contemporaries described her as an attractive woman with a strong personality. Photographs of the period show her to be in the Rubens tradition or as we would say in these politically correct times, "weight-enhanced".

I don't know what it was that she had, but whatever it was she must have had a lot of it, because in no time at all poor old Josiah Goode was swept off his feet. When the Holloway Company moved on, Madame Rowland stayed behind and Josiah set her up in a frock shop in one of his premises and installed her in the best room in the Exchange Hotel.

Mrs Goode quite naturally took a very dim view of these arrangements and it is recorded that during a fierce argument with Josiah one morning she threw a hot cup of tea over the aldermanic face. Josiah packed his bags and moved into the Exchange Hotel with Madame Rowland. The break was final and a deed of separation was drawn up whereby Mrs Goode was allowed use of the farm cottage and furniture and was to receive one hundred pounds a year - hardly a generous settlement when it was her capital that had been the base of the family fortune.

Josiah took to the drink again, neglected his aldermanic duties and in no time at all found himself on the receiving end of a typical "small town freeze" for his actions. Dubbo simply became too hot for the couple, so they moved to Molong where they opened a toy and fancygoods shop. As Josiah was seldom sober and Madame Rowland was no great shakes as a business entrepreneur, the venture was a disaster and they moved on to Melbourne, Madame Rowland's old home town. From there on it was downhill all the way.

Josiah's drinking problem became very serious indeed and the money was starting to run out. Back in Dubbo he had considerable holdings but they were heavily mortgaged and he refused to give his agents permission to sell any off, because the market was weak.

The cash flow from his agents virtually ceased and when he died suddenly on December 16, 1880 (of "general paralysis and softening of the brain" the doctor's certificate stated) the cupboard was bare of cash. Madame Rowland abandoned the body and poor old Josiah Goode (nominally one of Dubbo's richest men) was buried in a pauper's grave.

Josiah left two wills with distinctly conflicting intent, and they were both contested by the warring parties, Mrs Goode and Madame Rowland. In typical fashion the legal eagles of the day were able to spin out of the resulting cases for more than a quarter of a century, during which period both the female parties had died and the ultimate beneficiary, the Dubbo Base Hospital had entered the picture. In that time legal fees and mismanagement of the properties had reduced their value considerably.

When the Base Hospital finally got its inheritance in 1908 the estate had been reduced to the Exchange Hotel and the adjoining shops. And the Hospital Board, which had expended considerable funds in legal fees to get even that far, immediately found itself involved in controversy with sections of the community who maintained it was not appropriate for the hospital to own such an asset. After all, they said, down town the Hotel was giving its patrons all sorts of liver and other complaints that the Hospital ultimately was called on to patch up or cure!

That debate raged on for another sixty years while the hospital resisted outside pressures and was probably the only hospital in the world to own a hotel.

Finally, in 1968 they caved in, and sold the hotel and shops for a hundred and forty one thousand dollars and put the money towards building a new wing on the hospital. This they named THE JOSIAH GOODE MEMORIAL WING. They even put up a handsome plaque to mark the occasion, but the plaque makes no mention of the fact that old Josiah's bones are still mouldering in a pauper's grave in far off Melbourne.

We now come to the third example of our Dubbo Hiccups of History. This occurred in 1880 when the town was still in a high state of excitement over Josiah Goode's encampment with the mysterious Madame Rowland, and as news filtered back from Melbourne of his alcoholic decline in that fair city.

The focus of the 1880 Hiccup of History was the police magistrate, John Oxley Norton, who had been elevated to the bench after a long service in the police force. His only claim to fame in the service appears to have been the fact that in 1863, while he was serving under Frederick Pottinger in the southern district (see Chapter 7 Remittance Men), he was captured by Ben Hall the bushranger, and kept prisoner for three hours. This cheeky act by Ben Hall prompted the NSW Government to introduce the 1865 Felons Apprehension Act. The incident seems to have done no harm to Norton's career however, as soon after the event he was promoted to Sub-Inspector.

Norton appears to have been a very unsavoury character, if events in Dubbo are any guide. One of his early acts on the bench occurred in 1877 when he sentenced a man named Wilkie, who was at that time superintendent of a station in the Dubbo district, to three years hard labour on a sheep stealing charge. With Wilkie safely behind bars, Magistrate Norton then began an association with Wilkie's defacto, Catherine Wilkie (also known as Catherine Warren, or Mrs Mitchell —she appears to have had a somewhat dubious past).

Norton installed Catherine Wilkie quite openly as his Mistress in McCauley's Odd Fellows Arms Hotel, much to the great scandal of the more pious folk of the community. *The Dubbo Dispatch* was to later editorially comment that after Wilkie's gaoling " ... an illicit intimacy sprang up between (Norton) and this woman, which gradually became an infatuation on his part, despite the kindest and most persistent entreaties of his legion of loyal friends to break it off."

Norton may well have been infatuated with the attractive Catherine Wilkie, but that didn't prevent him treating her abominably, and physically assaulting her, especially when in the throes of drink, which seems to have been the magistrate's normal state.

The affair came to an abrupt end in a sensational manner on the afternoon of November 11 1880.

Now November 11 is a rather special day in Australian history. It was on that day in 1918 that World War I officially ended. Gough Whitlam and his Ministry had good cause to remember the remarkable events of November 11 1975, when they were sacked by the Governor General Sir John Kerr. And for Ned Kelly, November 11 1880, was the ultimate day of reckoning as on that morning he was hanged in Old Melbourne Gaol.

On that very day, in far off Dubbo another sensational event was brewing. In the afternoon Norton attended a political rally addressed by Sir Patrick Jennings, but left before it was over and, somewhat the worse for drink, arrived at McCauley's Hotel, where an altercation immediately occurred between himself and his mistress. There was nothing unusual about such scenes, which were a frequent pattern in the relationship, but on this occasion Catherine Wilkie decided that enough was enough. She took Norton's nickel plated Derringer from a drawer and shot him in the head. Norton was taken unconscious to the Dubbo Base Hospital where he lingered until December 26, before dying.

Catherine Wilkie was subsequently charged with murder, but was convicted on a lesser count of manslaughter, and sentenced to gaol for three years and a month. At the time of the shooting she had a two months old baby (presumably Norton's) and two other older children. No records survive of the fate of Catherine or the children in later years.

Norton's shooting and death caused a sensation, not only in Dubbo, but throughout Australia, since it isn't every day that a magistrate gets shot by his mistress in a country hotel love nest. The scandal sheets had a field day and the government of the day suffered intense embarrassment and much close scrutiny from an opposition delighted at having such a juicy scandal served up to it. And much of the criticism certainly was justified, since the government should have been aware of the existence of Norton's liaison with Wilkie as the affair was of long standing and the cause of considerable gossip and comment in the Dubbo community. It seems clear that a Government order went forth that replacement in Dubbo had to be someone of impeccable rectitude to avoid a recurrence of such a scandal.

The Boffins of the Justice Department looked around and came up with an answer that in itself led to a huge Hiccup in Australian history. Their choice for the Dubbo job was a chap named Browne, then serving as magistrate at Gulgong, where he also held the post of District Gold Commissioner. He had done something to offend the miners on the Gulgong goldfields and there was a petition circulating to have him removed. In posting him to Dubbo the Department solved two problems with the one action. They got him out of the hair of the Gulgong miners and it was certain that he would not cause any scandal in Dubbo since he was a married man with a large family of eight children.

To tell the truth, Thomas Alexander Browne was a fairly dull sort of fellow. He was born in London in 1826 and migrated to Australia with his parents when he was four years old. He had a good education in the Academy of WT Cape, in Sydney, the "right" school for sons of gentlemen of the colony. The family later moved to Victoria where Browne married, and engaged in two farming ventures which both failed. In 1870 he left the land and joined the NSW Public Service, being appointed to the Gulgong post the following year.

The transfer to Dubbo was an unwelcome move for Browne, since Gulgong was a more important town than Dubbo at that time, and he lost the bonus of the Gold Commissioner's salary. With a large family to keep it was tough making ends meet on the salary of a Police Magistrate so he turned his thoughts to ways of supplementing his income. He had dabbled in writing poetry and had a couple of short stories published (anonymously) so decided to have a go at writing another novel - his first attempt called *Ups and Downs* not having found favour with any publisher.

It is recorded that at six o'clock one cold and frosty morning he put quill to paper and started to write a tale about bushrangers. When he had completed several chapters he sent them off to two magazines in Sydney for appraisal but, ironically as it turned out, both magazines rejected them. Fortunately he persevered and, at the third attempt, the *Sydney Mail* decided to publish them in serialised format under the title *Robbery Under Arms*) using the pseudonym that Browne had chosen of Rolf Boldrewood.

Publication commenced in the *Sydney Mail* on July 1 1882, and it was from the start a sensational success, with excited readers forming queues outside newsagents each week to read of the latest adventures of Dick Marston as Captain Starlight (modelled on the real life bushranger known as 'Midnight'). Browne was hard put writing extra chapters between his work magistrate.

After the serialisation, *Robbery Under Arms* was published in book form in many editions, earning its author more than ten thousand pounds - a staggering sum for a 19th Century novelist. It was dramatised in the early 1900's and was the subject of four films over the years.

Browne went on to write fourteen other novels, none of which achieved the success of *Robbery Under Arms*, but all of which earned royalties because his name was attached to them. Even Mrs Browne attempted to climb aboard the gravy train in 1893 when she had published *The Flower Garden in Australia* by Mrs Rolf Boldrewood!

Robbery Under Arms not only brought fame and fortune to Browne the author, but it had important national spinoffs which have not always been recognised. It was translated into a dozen foreign languages and brought to readers in all parts of the globe some understanding of life in Australia, even though the tale was glamorised. Like no other piece of 19th Century writing, it put Australia "on the map" in a real international sense.

But, much more importantly, it gave tremendous hope and encouragement to a whole generation of Australian writers, men and women, striving to get their nationalistic feelings into print. If a rather dull, country magistrate could achieve this, then perhaps so could they. There is no way that we can measure the actual influence Browne had on such struggling writers as Lawson, Paterson and other bush oriented writers of the period, but success does breed further success and Browne's impact must surely have inspired many young writers to put pen to paper.

His books may not survive the test of time, but his achievement in actually writing them, and getting them into print, was an enormous inspiration to his generation.

And all because of a Hiccup of History when an angry young mistress shot a brutal magistrate in a country hotel.

3

The River Kings

Historians all too often seem to get their priorities wrong when selecting subjects for study and presentation. Take the case of Burke and Wills who led a publicly funded expedition for which they clearly lacked the experience and expertise. Because of this they ended up starving under a tree in the middle of nowhere, all within cooee of a large well fed tribe of aborigines.

Their upbringing and natural prejudices may have been the reason they did not seek help from what they would have regarded "these inferior people", help that almost certainly would have been forthcoming. For the aborigines had a long tradition of extending aid to non-threatening strangers in the land.

Academic careers have been built on, and forests of trees chopped down , recording the Burke and Wills saga, but if these two idiots had never set foot in Australia the history of the continent would not have changed one iota. They discovered nothing, achieved nothing and made no contribution to the development of the country in their rather useless lives. Yet historians have made them into legendary figures while totally ignoring the contributions of countless **real** pioneers such as John Egge or the McCulloch brothers whose names are not even mentioned in the ten volume *Australian Encyclopaedia* or the mainstream works of our top ranking historians. Why? Because they indulged in that lowly-status activity known as trade and commerce.

Let me tell you something about these three individuals who influenced the lives of many thousands of outback Australians and who brought more changes to the standards of living of these settlers than boatloads of Burkes and Wills ever could.

James and William McCulloch arrived on these shores from Scotland in 1852 and quickly saw the opportunities opening up as a result of the gold rushes then in their early stages. They applied their considerable talents and energies to developing a transport empire which within a decade had become the largest of its kind in the world.

At its peak their empire included more than twenty paddle steamers plying the Murray and Darling River systems, a fleet of coaches almost rivalling that of Cobb & Co, an extensive network of parcel delivery services in Melbourne and Adelaide and healthy shipping service and import/export agencies. By the sixties they dominated the inland trading networks of three states, Victoria, South Australia and New South Wales.

In the end they over-stretched their resources and came unstuck as a result of a combination of outside circumstances beyond their control: a prolonged drought, rapidly rising commercial interest rates which followed the land boom collapse and bank crashes of the 1880's and failure to appreciate the full extent of the impact of the burgeoning railways on their business.

The final straw that broke the camel's back in their case was the extension of the railway line from Dubbo to Bourke in 1884. Up to then McCulloch & Company had enjoyed a virtual monopoly of the carriage (and often selling) of the wool produced along the Darling River. This trade accounted for a substantial percentage of their income and profits. And they lost it all overnight with the coming of a railhead on the Darling as the woolgrowers immediately switched to this new transport system. This was not only cheaper but got their wool to market at a fraction of the time taken under the old system, which involved riverboat shipment to either Wentworth or Echuca, then long and slow bullock wagon hauls to Adelaide or Melbourne.

McCullochs went bust in a big way in 1886, losing their vast empire to the banks, though the McCulloch name lingered on in a smaller Adelaide carrying business for many years. When the collapse came two young men employed by the firm as clerks at Echuca suddenly found themselves out of a job with bleak prospects locally as the inland was then in the grip of drought and recession. They decided to pool resources and went to Melbourne where they acquired one of McCulloch's suburban parcel carrying services. They made a go of this venture and in time built it into their own empire. One of these chaps was named Mayne and the other was Nickless. Today the firm they founded straddles the world as a major security service giving a lot of meaning to the old saw that as one door closes, another opens - if you are smart enough to spot the opening!

As the McCulloch empire was waning along the Murray-Darling system, another enterprise was rising due to the astuteness of another migrant; one from a far different land from the Scottish Highlands from where the McCulloch's came. This newcomer on the scene was John Egge who was born in Shanghai in 1829 and who found employment, first as a cabin boy , then as cook, on one of the ships owned by Captain Francis Cadell, then plying the China trade. In 1852 he came to Australia on the Queen of Sheba when Cadell decided to turn his attention to the southern Australian coastal trade. Initially Cadell plied the Port Adelaide to Melbourne run, but later he helped pioneer the opening of the Murray River trade to take service to the many small settlements which had sprung up along the river following the gold boom of the early 1850's.

In 1855 John Egge was serving as cook on the river boat *Albury*, and in 1856 he was cook on the *Gundagai*, the first part-iron steamer on the inland river systems. On both boats he was registered in the crew list as 'John Bull' - a name he evidently considered unsatisfactory as in 1856 he changed his name by deed poll to John Egge (his original Chinese name is not known).

At that time he also deserted (for a time) the riverboat trade to try his luck on the land. First he bought land at Goolwa, but soon moved to Hindmarsh Island in Lake Alexandrina where he established a piggery - an unusual venture for a Chinaman in Australia at that time.

On the Victorian side of the river, almost opposite his holding, was another piggery established by a Cornishman named Perring. He was much interested in this rival operation from a practical point of view, but was even more interested in the Perrings' sixteen year old daughter Mary.

But there were difficulties attached to romantic ideas of this nature quite apart from the xenophobic antagonism being directed at all members of the "yellow race" at that time as a result of the flood of Chinese pouring into the Victorian goldfields. One practical difficulty was that the Murray was wide and swift flowing and that John Egge did not possess a boat to bridge the gap.

Not deterred by this, he would go down to the riverbank after a hard days work, undress and swim across with his clothes on his head, get dressed and go a-courting Mary Perring. He must have been a very persistent suitor because the Perrings eventually gave in and John Egge and Mary Perring were married on April 8 1857. The marriage appears to have been very successful and in the course of time produced eleven children.

But John Egge soon came to the conclusion that his small piggery would not support a growing family so in 1859 he boarded a passing trading ship signing on as cook and Mary as stewardess.

They disembarked at Wentworth, on the junction of the Murray and the Darling and then the largest settlement in the district. He went back to his old trade of cook and started to bake cakes and pies which he peddled around town each day in a basket. This was so successful that within a year he was able to open a bakery in the town. This followed over the years by the acquisition of a butchery, a boarding house and four hotels. By 1875 he was one of Wentworth's largest landowners, paying rates on more than a dozen properties, including a general trading store near the Wentworth wharf. In 1868 he had become naturalised.

But the lure of the river was ever present and he decided to lease a boat the *Teviot*. To operate this he required a licence, thus becoming Australia's first (and possibly only) Chinese riverboat captain.

The *Teviot* was only a small vessel of 19 tons, being 55 feet long, with a beam of 7 feet 8 inches. It had been built in Wahgunyah in 1865. Egge fitted this out as a supply vessel taking goods of various kinds from his Wentworth store up and down the river runs. In time he leased or bought five other vessels, all but one being ordinary cargo carrying boats.

The exception was to become his pride and joy and a great attraction along the whole Murray-Darling system. This was the *Murrumbidgee*, which he acquired in 1887 when the former McCulloch fleet came up for auction at Echuca. The *Murrumbidgee* was much larger boat than any others in the Egge fleet, being of 76 tons, 83 feet long with a beam of l6ft 6in and a draft of 4ft 6in. It had been built at Echuca in 1865.

John Egge fitted the *Murrumbidgee* out as a full-scale emporium, carrying a wide variety of clothing , furniture, household goods and farm implements of all types. There were changing cubicles, racks, counters, cash register etc. - a kind of floating David Jones or Myers!

The *Murrumbidgee* went up and down the river system to an established schedule, promoted in advance by newspaper advertisements and circulars so that settlers and their families came from miles around each staging; if the floating emporium did not have what a customer sought, details would be taken and it would invariably be on board next time around.

The *Murrumbidgee* and the *Teviot* were crisscrossing the Murray continually and this posed a problem. The Murray was the border between New South Wales and Victoria and each state levied landing charges for each docking; in the case of Victoria the docking fee was a hefty ten pounds. Of course many of the landing places were not manned by customs officers so Captain Legge was able to evade many of the charges, but the levies he was forced to pay each month (up to two thousand pounds in some busy months) were eating into his profits to such an extent that he organised giant petitions of customers on both sides of the river and presented his case as a service provider to the Riverland so forcefully that both New South Wales and Victorian governments waived the landing fees on his floating shops.

Captain John Egge became extremely wealthy from his many enterprises and may well have been the wealthiest Chinese resident of Australia in the latter part of the 19th Century. He was, in today's terms, certainly a multi-millionaire. But he was also noted right along the Riverland for his generosity to charitable causes and support of organisations in the towns where he traded.

He died in Wentworth in 1901, aged 72, and is buried in the special Egge section of the Wentworth Cemetery which contains four impressive free-standing headstones - one for his wife Mary who predeceased him in 1891, one for himself and one each for Mary's mother and father.

The large family that John and Mary Egge raised are now scattered around Australia - none remain in the Wentworth district to carry on his entrepreneurial enterprises. Two of his grandsons, Rupert Egge and William Egge, served in the AIF in World War 1, and many others made their mark in other fields.

Back in the 1980's one of his great grandsons travelled on his motor bike from Melbourne to Wentworth to research the family history with the idea of writing a book on his famous ancestor. Sadly he was killed in an accident on his way back to Melbourne with all the material he had gathered, so the project withered on the vine.

For my book Captain John Egge represents all the very best in Australia's rich multicultural history, a shining example to all our migrants no matter what corner of the globe they hail from. He was the ultimate Good Egge in our heady cultural pancake.

4

The Vaucluse Snakes

Without any doubt the most unusual (and eccentric) convict ever to be transported to Australia was Sir Henry Browne Hayes (1762-1832), a wealthy Irishman, and Sheriff of Cork, who landed on our shores as a result of a crazy escapade in which he took a short cut to the wooing of a Quaker heiress by simply kidnapping her!

Sir Henry came from a long established and respected Protestant family of the Munster, his father being Attiwell Hayes, a prominent social figure in the city of Cork. He was also much noted for his eccentric behaviour, a failing he passed on to his son Henry.

Henry was born with the proverbial silver spoon in his mouth, and honours came to him easily and early in life. In 1782 at the tender age of 20 he was admitted as a Freeman of the City of Cork and in 1790 he became one of the Sheriffs of the City. In that capacity he waited on and entertained the Lord Lieutenant to the city, for which he was knighted.

When Militia Regiments were formed, ostensibly to restore law and order but in reality to stamp out Catholic dissent, Sir Henry was appointed Captain in charge of the South Cork Regiment. This enabled him to strut his stuff in some style with his personal tent having a canopy of silk, a uniform with as many extra adornments as regulations permitted, and rosettes on BOTH sides of his cocked hat instead the usual custom of being attached only to one side. In other words he was a bit of a fashion plate, even a dandy.

Sir Henry led a full and active social life, fancied himself as an amateur actor, and entertained lavishly at his estate at Mt Vernon on the outskirts of Cork. He was also given to occasional hautiness, perhaps not unusual for one of his very considerable inherited wealth and social position. The only physical description we have of him is that he was about five feet seven inches with florid complexion, slightly pock-marked face, brown hair and long whiskers.

In 1797, at the age of 35, he found himself a widower "with numerous children" and apparently in need of a new wife. He set about the task of acquiring one in an extremely unorthodox manner.

The object of his attention was Miss Mary Pike, then aged 21, the daughter of a deceased banker of Cork, who had left her most of his fortune (over twenty thousand pounds - an enormous sum of money at that time). This legacy it seems caused serious divisions in the Pike family and, as is so often the case in such matters, religion was at the bottom of the upheaval. The Pikes had been one of the most prominent members of the Cork Quakers, but before his death the banker had had a serious falling out with the movement. He and his daughter Mary ceased to follow the Quaker cause, while Mrs Pike and other family members remained in the fold, which probably explains the inheritance.

After her father's death, Mary moved out of the family home and went to live with her uncle, Mr Cooper Penrose, on his showpiece estate "Woodhill", some miles from the city. The Penroses had a daughter (her cousin) about Mary's age so she seemed quite content to be living at "Woodhill".

The only description of Mary Pike to come down to us describes her as "comely", but given her fortune of twenty thousand pounds plus, this appeared to be no handicap as far as Sir Henry was concerned. She may well have been comely but she certainly had plenty of spirit and intelligence. This shone through at the subsequent trial when she was subjected to lengthy cross-examination. The transcripts showed clearly that she held her end up without turning a hair even under the most persistent questioning by learned counsel.

Sir Henry motives for setting his cap at Mary Pike were not raised at the trial but we may assume that her inheritance would have had some bearing on the matter, though Sir Henry does not seem to have been in any financial difficulty, then or later, judging by the way he splashed money around for the next couple of decades.

What is puzzling is his method of courtship, if that term can be applied to what followed. After all Sir Henry was at that time in his prime, a Knight of the realm, wealthy in his own right and a very prominent figure in Cork society. He was a "catch" by any standard, especially for a comely maiden who was then past the usual marriagable age.

Sir Henry may have been deterred from undertaking an orthodox courtship by Mary's background. In her teens she had incurred her father's displeasure by falling in love with one of his bank clerks, a young fellow named Cleburne, who was distantly related to the Pikes. Old man Pike nipped that romance in the bud but local gossip had it that there had been other suitors, some prominent, who had been rejected out of hand by Mary. Maybe she was still pining over young Cleburne and, knowing this, Sir Henry did not want to risk similar rejection.

Whatever the reason, the alternate method of courtship chosen by Sir Henry was bizarre in the extreme. He concocted a plan to kidnap Mary Pike and marry her by force, even though up to that time he had never set eyes on her! And this was no wild impulsive move but a carefully planned and executed scheme requiring the assistance of a number of accomplices, including his own sister and a priest (or at least someone claiming to be a priest), as well as at least four and possibly five members of his household entourage.

It is probable that Sir Henry dreamed up this wildly improbable scheme as a result of hearing of a similar plot carried out a century earlier in the reign of Charles II. The perpetrator on that occasion was the Earl of Rochester who abducted a Miss Meillon and caused His Majesty so much displeasure that he had to make himself scarce from the kingdom for a while. But that adventure did have a happy ending as two years later Miss Meillon had a change of heart and agreed to marry the impetuous Earl. No such luck came Sir Henry's way in his well planned enterprise.

And the planning and execution was impeccable - if only the lady concerned had been a bit more flexible in her attitude, all might have ended as happily as the Earl's venture. But this was not to be.

Sir Henry's planning had to overcome several obstacles. One was to find a way of enticing Mary Pike away from the clutches of the Penrose family. Sir Henry's plan was to use Mary's mother as bait for the trap he set. Mrs Pike still lived in the family home in Cork with her elder daughter (Mary's half-sister) and was known to be in ill health. Although Mary had been estranged from her mother since her father's death, Sir Henry reasoned (correctly) that she would respond to an urgent call to her mother's deathbed.

How to arrange this? Why a letter from the family doctor delivered in the middle of the night. And it was here that Sir Henry displayed some skill in the ancient art of skulduggery. The Pike family doctor in Cork was Dr Robert Gibbings, who was known to Sir Henry only by repute. Sir Henry sent the doctor a note requesting some information on a matter he knew to be in the doctor's field of interest. When the reply came he was then in possession of a copy of the doctor's handwriting, which he proceeded to practice until he felt he could produce a note which would pass muster in the middle of the night.

His next problem was to actually identify his intending bride. As he had never laid eyes on her he didn't want to abduct the wrong person, so he decided to pay a visit to the Penrose estate to identify her, and no doubt assure himself that she was presentable enough to be the future Lady Hayes.

"Woodhill" was a magnificent estate with some fifty acres of gardens and trees, a showpiece of the district which attracted many visitors. Some years before Sir Henry had inspected the gardens when he was upgrading the gardens in his own estate, and had met Cooper Penrose on that occasion, but had not been invited into the house.

On his bridal survey mission he made his visit in the afternoon and Cooper Penrose showed him around the gardens, Sir Henry, who was a great talker, managed to spin the visit out until the dinner bell rang, when Cooper felt obliged to invite him in for dinner, An invitation that was quickly accepted. The Cooper's had other guests that evening and Mary Pike and the two Penrose daughters sat at a side table, but Sir Henry no doubt saw enough to convince him that the time had come to set his master plan in motion.

Some three weeks later, in the early hours of Saturday, July 22

1797, the plan was put into execution with military precision. Around one o'clock in the morning, when most, but not all the Penrose household were abed, a messenger arrived with a letter, supposedly from Dr Gibbings, reading: "To Cooper Penrose, esq. Dr Sir, Our Friend, Mrs Pike, is taken suddenly ill: she wishes to see Miss Pike; we would recommend dispatch, as we think she has not many hours to live, your's, &c. Robt Gibbings".

Cooper Penrose, who did not question the authenticity of the note, immediately aroused the household and had a carriage prepared. In pouring rain this set off for Cork bearing Mary Pike, a relative, Mrs Pike, wife of Richard Pike of Cork, Miss Anne Penrose, and the driver and a footman.

On the Glanmire road the coach was held up by at least five horsemen, including Sir Henry wearing a handkerchief over the lower part of his face as a disguise. Sir Henry forced Mary out of the carriage and into another carriage nearby occupied by a woman (subsequently identified as Sir Henry's sister). After cutting the traces and turning loose the horses of the Penrose carriage (thus stranding the occupants), the waiting coach and the riders set off for Sir Henry's estate at Mount Vernon. There, because of the pouring rain, they had problems getting the coach up the steep driveway, so Sir Henry carried the struggling and protesting Mary up the drive and into his house.

There in a dimly lighted room she was confronted with a man dressed as a priest who proceeded to conduct a marriage ceremony partly in French and partly in heavily accented English Mary couldn't understand. A ring was forced on to her finger and Sir Henry told her that she was now legally Lady Hayes. Mary wouldn't have a bar of that and taking the ring from her finger hurled it across the room.

Sir Henry had a problem. He tried to solve this by drawing a revolver, putting it to his head and threatening to shoot himself on the spot if Mary didn't give in. His bluff didn't work and Mary was taken upstairs and locked in a room containing only a bed and a desk.

Later Sir Henry brought his new bride supper and tried to talk her around but all his efforts were in vain. He finally capitulated and allowed her to write a note to the Penroses, explaining where she was. At that stage Sir Henry must have realised that he was in deep trouble - up a creek without a paddle as it were. He and his sister simply did a quick vanishing act.

Mary's note was delivered to the Penroses in the morning and they quickly arrived at Mount Vernon to collect her. The weekend was spent in family consultation and on Monday Mary was taken to the Cork Police Station where she signed a deposition and laid formal charges against Sir Henry.

News of the kidnapping quickly spread and caused a sensation in Cork where Sir Henry was so well known. The populace appeared to be pretty solidly on Sir Henry's side in what was widely but mistakenly believed to be a lovers' tiff. The street bulletins, forerunners to today's scandal press, had a field day, often breaking out into outrageous comments and verse such as:

> Sir Henry kissed behind the bush,
> Sir Henry kissed the Quaker,
> And if he did, and if he did,
> I'm sure he didn't ate her.

And this terrible effort:

> The fate of Sir Henry is sure a hard case,
> Unable in Cork to exhibit his face,
> Pursued by the brethren, proclaimed in the papers,
> Though his mighty misdeed were mere boyish capers;
> Since Mercy, high Goddess, re-visits these climes,

And rebels and traitors are pardon'd their crimes,
Tho' different his guilt let them all share alike,
He was not United and gave up his Pike.

The police initially seemed to be very reluctant to pursue what they considered a domestic matter, especially as Mary Pike had not suffered any physical harm, and their search for the missing Sir Henry was not conducted with diligence even when the government posted a reward of five hundred pounds for his arrest. The Pike family upped the ante by offering a further five hundred pounds. Despite the fact that a thousand pounds was a huge sum in those days,no one turned Sir Henry in. In fact public sentiment was so much against Mary Pike, probably on religious grounds as much as anything else, she felt forced to leave Cork and went to live with relatives in England.

After several months Sir Henry felt it safe enough to return to Cork and take up residence at Mt Vernon. After sniffing the wind he then boldly and openly re-entered the rounds of social life in the city. The police appeared to be uninterested in executing the arrest warrants being held against their former Sheriff.

It seems incredible but almost two years passed in this fashion before Sir Henry had another bright idea which almost put a noose around his neck. Feeling that public opinion was so much on his side that no Cork jury would convict him, he decided to give himself up and face the legal music. But the method he chose was unusual to say the least. In Cork a former family employee named Coghlan had set himself up as a hairdresser and perfumer. Sir Henry visited Coghlan and suggested that he accompany him along to the police station and "turn him in". This was done, Sir Henry was arrested and in due course Coghlan received the combined rewards of a thousand pounds and built himself three red brick houses on the Grand Parade of Cork, thus ensuring himself considerable prosperity in his retirement years.

Sir Henry was not so lucky. When the case came before the Cork Court on April 13 1801, Sir Henry found himself pitted against a formidable legal duo in the shape of Judge Day, who had a reputation for tough sentencing, and as chief prosecuting counsel J. P. Curran, one of the most brilliant Irish advocates of the 19th Century. Curran's final address to the jury was such a masterpiece of convincing logic that the jury took only an hour to bring in a verdict of guilty - but with a recommendation tor mercy. Sir Henry was profoundly shocked when he was condemned to death, but on appeal the sentence was commuted to transportation for life. Which is how we came to acquire our first titled convict.

But Sir Henry did not come to our shores quite like that of so many thousands of his fellow convicts in that era. He came in some style aboard the convict ship *Atlas*, accompanied by a veritable mountain of luggage, and wined and dined throughout the tiresome voyage at the Captain's table. He achieved this by paying a considerable sum (said to be three hundred guineas) to Captain Brookes.

At each port of call the captains of all convict ships were required to put all convicts in chains for the full period of the ship's stay. Such indignity was not for Sir Henry who was allowed to go ashore sightseeing at each port of call. After one such excursion in Rio, Sir Henry returned to the ship to find Captain Brookes engaged in a brawl on the quarter deck with one of the government passengers, Surgeon Jamieson, who according to Sir Henry, was very drunk. The gallant Sir Henry came to the rescue of the beleagured Captain and separately the sparring couple, apparently using some force. In his account of the event, Sir Henry noted: "Our kindness procured us all, and me in particular, a volley of abuse in terms not calculated to escape notice. On the shore the next day, when the fumes of liquor were dissipated, I requested an apology, and obtained satisfaction. The steps I then took were those universally approved of. He went on board another ship and I forgot him."

But Sir Henry's satisfaction was short-lived. He may have forgotten Surgeon Jamieson, but Jamieson had certainly not forgotten Sir Henry. And the ship he had transferred to was a faster vessel than the Atlas and reached Sydney before it.

When the *Atlas* arrived on July 6 1802, an unpleasant surprise awaited Sir Henry. He found Jamieson installed in the post of acting chief surgeon and magistrate, and out for vengeance over the Rio incident. Sir Henry was confined to the ship for two weeks then taken ashore and charged with assaulting the Chief Surgeon at Rio. He was sentenced to six months imprisonment and actually served five months before being released and sent to Parramatta under threat of being sent to Norfolk Island if he returned to Sydney Town where his luggage and goods were stored. Sir Henry ignored these threats and was soon back in Sydney to claim his belongings, set up house and generally make a nuisance of himself by consorting with Irish Catholics such as Edward Redmond, who had been transported for rebellion in 1798. Governor Gidley King suspected him of being involved in the Parramatta plotting which led to the uprising and battle of Vinegar Hill in 1804 but he could not prove anything and no charges were brought against Sir Henry.

However, if Sir Henry was busy plotting with the Catholics, he didn't forget his Protestant origins and organised a Masonic Lodge. Governor King banned the new organisation but Sir Henry went ahead anyway and presided over the first Masonic meeting to be held on Australian soil. Constables raided the meeting and arrested everyone present. Next day the magistrates acquitted everyone except Sir Henry who they ordered to be exiled to the new settlement in Van Dieman's Land, but this sentence was never enforced - or Sir Henry managed to bribe his way out of it, the records are far from clear on such matters.

Meanwhile Sir Henry was using his extensive fortune to dabble in Sydney real estate. On April 18 1803 he purchased from Elizabeth Bradshaw a house in Chapel Row, along with a boat, and some timber, for the sum of twenty seven pounds seven shillings. The reference to the boat on the receipt of purchase is interesting. All the early governors had clear instructions that they were not to permit boat building of any kind in the colony because it was feared that the convicts would steal them and sail them away to China! Since Sydney at this time was landlocked, no way having been found across the Blue Mountains, all the early governors ignored the Whitehall instruction since it would have impeded communications up and down the coastline. Yet here was one of the colony's most notorious convicts, suspected of plotting the overthrow of authority, openly buying a boat. The Mandarins of Whitehall would have had kittens had they been aware of the transaction.

At auction on August 22 1803, Sir Henry made a much larger purchase when he acquired for one hundred pounds two farms known as Laycock Farm and Cardal Farm, near South Head, from the estate of the late Captain Thomas Dennett, the auctioneer being Simeon Lord, one of the noted Sydney traders.

Sir Henry amalgamated the two farms and re-named his new estate Vaucluse, thus giving a name to what was to become one of Sydney's most prestigious suburbs.

On this estate he built a quite imposing house, the first Vaucluse House, part of which was later incorporated into the much larger and grander Vaucluse House which survives to the present. The house had two large wings , one twenty seven feet by twenty feet and the other twenty four feet by ten feet. The total cost, including outhouses, sheds and landscaping was a shade over seventeen hundred pounds. This did not include an extra twenty pounds which Sir Henry later spent providing a roadway for the half mile from the house to the Highway (ie. Old South Head Road) . The total area of the new Vaucluse estate was one hundred and five acres - all acquired at a total all up costs of land, buildings and road somewhat under two thousand pounds.

Sir Henry lost no time moving into his new estate, certainly the most palatial ever held by a serving convict, and immediately turned to his favourite occupation - throwing parties. But life at Vaucluse House had its problems, not the least being the plague of snakes on the property. He put up with them for a while but decided to put a halt to their activities after they started to invade the house and his bed. Recalling that Saint Patrick had banished snakes from Ireland and that the reptiles were said to abhor Irish bog, Sir Henry ordered from Ireland five hundred barrels of the stuff. When they arrived he had workmen dig a trench six feet wide and two feet deep right around the house and into this trench he had the men - Irish convicts one and all - consign the Irish bog.

And it worked! We have impeccable testimony to this fact from the pen of the redoubtable Reverend John Dunmore Lang himself, who in his book *Botany Bay*, told the story and noted: "Strange to say, from that time forward, Sir Henry Hayes was not visited by snakes. They did not vacate the ground in the vicinity of Vaucluse, but none were ever seen within the magic circle formed by the Irish earth... Captain Piper assured me that during the many years he lived there with his family, no venomous reptile had ever been killed or observed within Hayes' enclosures notwithstanding they were plentiful enough beyond it."

But if Sir Henry had solved the snake problem at Vaucluse House, he continued to fall foul of authority, mainly in the form of Governor King with whom he appears to have had a running feud. In 1806 Governor King banished Sir Henry and another Irish convict to Norfolk Island.

After they had been there a month, the Governor evidently had second thoughts about sending what he considered a pair of Irish plotters to the same place. He gave instructions that Sir Henry was to be transferred to Port Dalrymple. On this occasion Sir Henry's luck held out as the ship carrying him to Port Dalrymple, the Buffalo, encountered such heavy weather after leaving Norfolk Island that it was forced to put into Port Jackson for shelter and somehow Sir Henry managed to talk (or bribe) his way ashore and stay there. At least for the time being.

When Gidley King was replaced by Governor Bligh, harmony returned to his life. For once he was in tune with authority as he and Bligh got along famously. But again Sir Henry had backed the wrong horse as when Bligh was overthrown in the infamous Rum Rebellion of 1808, he was on the blacklist again and promptly exiled to Newcastle.

This outpost was governed by Lieutenant Lawson, who proceeded to make life very difficult for the titled convict. On one occasion Lawson had Sir Henry thrown into the guard house while he proceeded to raid his house in search of incriminating documents. He didn't find any.

But Sir Henry's long travail on our shores was coming to a close.

On April 10 1809, while the deposed Governor Bligh was being held under house arrest he prepared a pardon for Sir Henry Hayes, but this could not be issued as he had no access to the Great Seal. When Bligh eventually returned to England he forwarded a copy of the pardon to the Earl of Liverpool, explained the circumstances and requested that Sir Henry be released. Lord Liverpool immediately forwarded this request on to Governor Lachlan

Macquarie for execution.

Sir Henry Browne Hayes left Sydney on December 4 1812, on the Isabella in company with another prominent convict exile, "General" Joseph Holt. The Isabella was wrecked at the Falkland Islands in February 1813, but there was no loss of life and the pair of distinguished exiles eventually reached Dublin, "General" Holt to trade as a publican and Sir Henry to take up residence at 35 Dawson Street, Dublin, "to live on his money" - as one magazine at the time put it. The same magazine made the witty comment: "It is singular enough that the two were transported for the Pike business. Sir Henry was transported for stealing a Pike, and the "General" for bestowing Pikes".

Sir Henry did not linger long in Dublin but soon returned to his beloved Cork. Ainsworth's Magazine described him thus: "A portly person, wearing striped trousers and a blue coat with brass buttons, having a rubicund face, charged with effrontery, and shaded by the broad leaf of a straw sombrero".

In Cork, Sir Henry took up residence in Thomas Street, being blind in his latter years. He died in May 1832, aged 70, at his then residence on Grantham Hill. Recording the death, the Cork Constitution of May 1832 noted: "He sustained a very sincere illness for many months with pious resolution; he was kind and indulgent parent, and a truly adherent friend. The suavity and gentlemanly manner he possessed made him endeared to every person who had the honour of his acquaintance."

Sir Henry's many trials and tribulations in the Antipodes obviously did not deter other members of his family from venturing Down Under. One of his daughters married John Burnett, who with their nine children in tow arrived in Hobart in 1826 to become Colonial Secretary of Van Dieman's Land. It was a controversial appointment and Burnett was ultimately declared unfit for office by the Colonial Office.

In 1826 Sir Henry's nephew, Attwell Edwin Hayes also migrated to Australia and eventually founded the *Australasian* newspaper.

Sir Henry's story is an extraordinary one. He certainly had many ups and downs in his three score years and ten, but one can't but help feeling, that most of the "downs" were brought about by his own foolishness and impetuosity.

In the end, the question that must be asked is: Why, oh why, didn't he simply propose to Mary Pike in the normal manner? She may even have ended up saying "yes"!

5

Martial Law

The Proclamation of Martial Law is a very serious act only to be contemplated in times of extreme emergency, since all normal laws are suspended and all power passes to the military forces of the state for the duration of the proclamation period. So serious a matter is it, that the last time Martial Law was proclaimed in England was away back in 1628. Yet Martial Law was proclaimed **five times** in Australia in colonial times, and on three of these occasions the proclamation itself was illegal because the Proclaimer did not have the authority to act!

Let us look at these proclamations in chronological order:

1. In 1790 when the *Sirius* was wrecked off Norfolk Island the officer in charge of the garrison on the Island, Major Ross, fearful that convicts would escape and loot the wreck, proclaimed Martial Law, justifying his act in these terms: "Immediately on the ship's striking, I judged it necessary to issue an order forbidding all the inhabitants on the settlement from killing any stock of their own, or plundering any

article of stock or provisions belonging to the public or to others, under pain of immediate death by hanging." This proclamation was illegal since Major Ross had no authority to issue it.

2. In 1804 Governor Philip Gidley King proclaimed Martial Law during the brief insurrection of Irish convicts (and settlers) at Parramatta - an insurrection that was promptly quashed in the so-called Battle of Vinegar Hill. This proclamation was legal as King had such powers under his warrant as Governor.
3. In 1815 Lieutenant Governor Davey declared Martial Law in Van Diemen's Land to enable his troops to round up and shoot a band of escaped convicts. This proclamation was illegal as Davey being only a Lieutenant Governor, had no authority to so act.
4. In 1824 Governor Thomas Brisbane declared Martial Law in the Bathurst District of New South Wales (more anon.) This was a legal proclamation as Brisbane did have such powers, even though he abused his powers by maintaining the proclamation for a remarkable period of four months.
5. In 1854 Governor Charles Latham proclaimed Martial Law in Victoria (then a separate colony from New South Wales) during the Eureka Stockade incident. This was an illegal proclamation because the British Government had in 1837 withdrawn the right to proclaim Martial Law from all Governors, as a direct result of Brisbane's misuse of that power at Bathurst in 1824.

Let us look at this 1824 Bathurst proclamation in some detail since it is an incident that has received little attention in historical records. And to do this it is necessary to retrace our steps to put the act into its proper perspective.

For the first quarter of a century of its existence, the tiny convict colony of Sydney Town remained landlocked between the sea and the formidable Blue Mountains. That situation changed dramatically in 1813 when Blaxland, Lawson and Wentworth made their historic crossing of the Blue Moutains to discover vast fertile lands westward. After that the dynamic Governor Lachlan Macquarie saw to it that things moved at a brisk pace. In 1814 Lieutenant William Cox, with only thirty hand-picked convicts as his work force , achieved a minor miracle by constructing a rough but trafficable road of 105 miles across the mountains from Penrith to the present site of Bathurst.

Macquarie himself travelled across the mountains in 1815 to proclaim the village of Bathurst, where a small outpost garrison had been established. He also made a few land grants, approximately half going to Emancipists (ex-convicts) and half to Exclusionists (Free Settlers). His go-slow policy on land settlement was deliberate, designed to ensure that grants were made only to responsible settlers who would cause minimum problems with the numerous aborigines settled in the area.

The Bathurst aborigines were members of the widely dispersed Wiradjuri tribe whose territory extended in the north to the present site of Gunnedah, in the west to Nyngan and south to Hay. The word "tribe" is a loose description, covering numerous small extended family groupings with shared ancestry. In Macquarie's day the numbers throughout the Bathurst district were estimated at between 600 and 700. They thus far outnumbered the whites (soldiers, settlers and convicts). In the 1820 census the total (white) population west of the mountains numbered only 114, of which 75 were convicts.

Though the aborigines were numerous, they were not troublesome, at least in the early period. Macquarie in his notes on the Bathurst visit said they showed a degree of fear when first encountered, "but soon appeared to be reconciled on being kindly spoken to." He went on to observe: " They were all clothed with Mantles made of the skins of opossums which were very neatly sewn together and the outside of the skins were carved in a remarkably neat manner. They appeared to be very inoffensive and cleanly in their persons."

Major A. C. Antill, ADC. to the Governor recorded similar impressions: "They appear to be a harmless and inoffensive race, with nothing forbidding or ferocious in their countenance."

No problems with the aborigines were recorded in the remainder of Macquarie's term, due in large part to his practice of hand-picking settlers for the new outpost, settlers such as George Suttor who took the trouble to learn the language of the natives and who maintained good relations with them.

All that changed with the departure of Macquarie and the arrival of his successor, Governor Sir Thomas Macdougall Brisbane. Whereas Macquarie was a "hands-on" Governor taking a keen interest in every detail of the colony's administration, Brisbane was a weak and indecisive individual interested in little apart from his hobby of astronomy. The Reverend Samuel Marsden perhaps best summed him up in private letters he wrote to a fellow clergyman, the Reverend J Pratt. Of Brisbane, he said: "Amiable but weak disposition displayed by evading the exercise of his power..." and later, "Of amiable private character but totally unsuited as Governor New South Wales; has given authority to others."

In this last comment Marsden hit the nail on the head. In his aloofness from the day to day running of the colony, he left virtually everything to his Colonial Secretary, Frederick Goulburn, who probably was the real villain of the piece when it comes to apportioning blame for the tragedy of the Bathurst massacres of 1824.

Frederick Goulburn (1788-1837), described by John Macarthur as a "cold and selfish character" who "operated by deception and evasion", was the son of Munbee Goulburn of Portland Place, London, and younger brother of the Right Hon. Henry Goulburn, who was Secretary for the Colonies, and after whom Goulburn Plains was named in 1818.

The younger Goulburn was appointed a cornet in the 23rd Dragoons at the age of 17 and was present at the battle of Waterloo. He later became a Major in the 59th Regiment. No doubt due to the good offices of his brother, he was appointed Colonial Secretary to the colony of New South Wales in 1820, arriving on our shores on December 31 of that year.

Goulburn was largely responsible for implementing a new land policy which saw most of the western land grants awarded to the "gentry" (the Exclusionists). This lead to almost instant problems in the Bathurst area, since the gentrified landholders were mainly absentee landlords who relied on overseers to run their distant properties. These overseers often were ill-equipped for the job, sometimes quite disreputable characters unable or unwilling to control the convicts assigned to them.

Trouble arose in several ways. The new wave of settlement meant the aborigines were pushed further and further off their traditional hunting grounds, making conflict inevitable. But perhaps most trouble occurred over the treatment of aboriginal women who were regarded as "fair game" both by the soldiers of the garrison and the convict herdsmen. When the aborigines struck back by attacking and sometimes burning the huts of the herdsmen, the latter retaliated with the old tried and proven trick of leaving around the hut dampers laced with arsenic.

Perhaps the biggest problem resulted from the action of the white settlers in giving guns to their convict herdsmen in defiance of the terms under which the convicts were supplied for labour. Things came to a head when a party of six armed convicts hunted down a group of aborigines including a woman and two young girls. When the crime came to light, five of the six convicts were charged with manslaughter and taken to Sydney for trial. Despite a clear direction from the judge that they were guilty of the crime on the evidence presented, the jury returned a verdict of Not Guilty. This caused considerable outrage in Old Sydney Town and focussed a lot of attention on the sorry state of affairs regarding race relations in the Bathurst district. During the controversy that erupted it was disclosed that up to 1824 seven whites (all convicts) had been killed by aborigines. The number of aborigines killed was not known.

Clearly something had to be done. The plan of action, probably the brainchild of Goulburn, was nothing short of a tragedy.

On August 14 1824 Governor Brisbane proclaimed Martial Law throughout the District of Bathurst. He did this after an earlier request to Earl Bathurst, Secretary of the Colonies, unsuccessfully seeking permission to raise a Troop of Cavalry to keep order in Bathurst district. Brisbane justified his action in proclaiming Martial Law in these words: "Mutual Bloodshed may be stopped by the Use of Arms against the Natives beyond the ordinary Rule of Law in Time of Peace; and, for this End, Resort to summary Justice has become necessary".

To enforce this proclamation, the only act of Martial Law used against aborigines in Australian colonial history, Major Morisset, the Commandment of the Bathurst garrison , was given a free hand

and 75 men from the 40th Regiment. Neither Brisbane or Goulburn considered it necessary to go to Bathurst to determine how their directions were being implemented.

What then happened was outlined by Brisbane in a dispatch to Earl Bathurst, some time after the event:

"I found it necessary to augment the Detachment of Bathurst to 75 men, these were divided into various small parties, each headed by a magistrate, and proceeded in various directions towards the interior of the country and by previous arrangements were to form junctions at certain given points. This system of keeping these unfortunate people in a constant state of alarm, soon brought them to a sense of their duty."

Brisbane was lying through his teeth, trying to put a gloss on things and trying to save his own neck. For a start it is hardly likely that each party was headed by a magistrate since colonial magistrates were very thin on the ground in 1824, especially west of the mountains. Brisbane concealed the fact that his raiding parties comprised not only soldiers, but settlers and armed convicts. And he completely concealed the fact that the real purpose of the raiding parties was not to frighten the natives, but to shoot them on sight.

A much truer picture of what **really** happened is provided by on-the-spot observers. Writing in *Australian Stories Retold*, W H Suttor, drew upon the recollections of his father George Suttor who was an eye-witness to the events of 1824. He wrote:

"...the blacks were shot down without any respect. Getting the worst of it, most of them made out out into the deep dells of the Capertee country and although some escaped, many were killed there ...when Martial Law had run its course extermination is the word that most aptly describes the result. The last effort of a doomed race thus ended".

There were individual accounts of massacres of small groups of men, women and children, shot down indiscriminately at Billiwillinga, Bell's Falls gorge and Clear Creek.

Since the raiding parties did not keep any records, nobody knows how many aborigines were exterminated on the killing fields of Bathurst in that dreadful campaign. George Suttor thought the number was "several hundred" and this figure is supported by the Reverend W Walker, A Wesleyan missionary, who wrote to the General Secretary of the Wesleyan Mission, from the Native Settlement, on September 14 1814, exactly a month after the proclamation of Martial Law , commenting: "From the most satisfactory sources I think that not fewer than a hundred blacks, men, women and children, have been butchered". Since Martial Law had a further three months to run, the end total must have been considerably higher than this preliminary estimate yet when it was all over Brisbane wrote to Earl Bathurst, again lying in his teeth saying that he had not been able to ascertain the number of aborigines killed but he thought the number would not have been more than double the number of whites previously killed, that is fourteen!

If the estimates of aborigine numbers in the Bathurst area (600 to 700 in 1815) and George Suttor's estimates of several hundred killed are correct, then it is clear that at least a third of the Wiradjuri people were exterminated on the killing fields of Bathurst in an officially sanctioned act of genocide.

But not all the Wiradjuri groups were slaughtered and among the survivors of this campaign were the tribal group led by a chieftain named Windradyne, known to the district whites as "Saturday". He seems to have been targeted right from the start of the campaign because on August 18, only four days after the proclamation of Martial Law. Brisbane put a price on Windradyne's head when he issued a Government Notice: "Five hundred acres of land to be given to any Person who will bring in Saturday, alive, to any Magistrate of the territory. By his Excellency's Command." F Goulburn, Colonial Secretary.

A week later, a further notice was issued by Brisbane in which Saturday was identified as "supposed to have been a Principal Actor in the late murders committed on the White People, at Bathurst". The reward of five hundred acres of land was repeated but this notice omitted all reference to it being for a LIVE Saturday. The reward was for him dead or alive.

Despite the richness of this reward Windradyne proved to be an elusive quarry as he was not captured until late in November when he was surprised in his camp, overpowered and taken to Bathurst in chains.

The capture of Windradyne (Saturday) seems to have put an end to resistance by the Wiradjuri and on December 11 1824, after four months of upheaval and bloodshed, Governor Brisbane repealed the Proclamation of Martial Law, thus ending one of the most disgraceful episodes in the colony's history.

Back in August apparently Brisbane and Goulburn thought Windradyne such a villain that they were prepared to put a price on his head. But, having captured him, apparently they could not mount a case against him that would stand up, because they released him and invited him to attend the annual Feast of Honour for aboriginal chiefs, a practice that had been initiated by Governor Macquarie. In 1824 this was held at the Market Place in Parramatta on Tuesday, December 28, when Brisbane and his staff met and mingled with some several hundred aboriginal men, women and children including Windradyne and other surviving Bathurst chiefs.

Reporting the occasion, *The Sydney Gazette* of December 30, noted: " ...what contributed to give peculiar interest to the scene was the circumstance of the noted Saturday, the Bathurst chief, being at the head of his tribe. He is one of the finest looking natives we have seen in this part of the country. He is not particularly tall but much stouter and more proportionable limbed than the majority of his countrymen; which combined with a noble looking countenance and piercing eye, are calculated to impress the beholder with other than disagreeable feelings towards a character who has been so much dreaded by the Bathurst settler. Saturday is, without doubt, the most manly black native we have ever beheld - a fact pretty generally acknowledged by the numbers that saw him."

The Sydney Gazette scribe noted that Saturday wore a straw hat on which was affixed a label with the word "Peace" inserted. He also noted that when His Excellency retired from the scene after conversing with each Chief, the black throng arose to cheer the donor of their feast but "we observed the Bathurst forces were so intent on paying becoming respect to the repast, that they considered one cheer quite enough." And rightly so, in the light of recent events in their home territory!

In his subsequent dispatch to Earl Bathurst on the Parramatta conference, Governor Brisbane wrote: " ...I am most happy to have it in my power to report to Your Lordship that Saturday, their great and warlike chieftain, has been with me to receive his pardon, and that he with most of his tribe, attended the Annual Conference."

If Brisbane thought this bit of genuflecting to the Great One in Whitehall was going to save his skin he was greatly mistaken. Earl Bathurst had been receiving reports from various sources in Sydney Town about the four month long Martial Law campaign in the district which bore his name, and he didn't like what was being reported. In separate dispatches he was firstly, extremely critical of (and then sacked) Major Morisset, the Commander of the Bathurst

Garrison for "neglect of duty", sacked and recalled to London the Colonial Secretary, Frederick Goulburn, and in the bluntest of terms sacked Brisbane: "I am commanded by the King to signify to you that his Majesty is pleased to relieve you from the exercise of the Government of New South Wales."

So, in a way, a rough sort of justice was meted out to the three major villains of the piece, though their punishment was hardly commensurate with the sufferings they inflicted on the unfortunate Wiradjuri people of the Bathurst district. No doubt a prosecution could have been mounted against all three but that would have involved public hearings and the airing of much soiled linen in public. Those who control the matters of state invariably prefer to sweep such scandals under the carpet.

In due course Ex-Governor Brisbane left the colony and retired to Scotland where he resumed his studies of astronomy and acquired some minor fame in scientific circles for his efforts. He died in 1860.

Major Frederick Goulburn returned to London to face the music. There, no doubt due to the influence of his brother and family, he was thrashed over the knuckles with a feather and given a minor posting in Ireland. He died in 1837.

Major Morisset who did all the dirty work in the field for his Sydney masters, fared better. After doing some penance in England he was allowed to return to the colony in 1826 and eventually became Commandant at Norfolk Island where he acquired a reputation as a stern disciplarian, resulting in several unsuccessful mutiny attempts on the part of his convict charges. He resigned from the army in 1838 and purchased a farm at Winburndale Brook, near Bathurst, and was appointed a police magistrate on a salary of three hundred pounds a year. He died in 1852, aged 72.

Windradyne continued to lead his tribe for a good few years

after the unhappy events of 1824, and appears to have avoided in this period the fate which befell so many of his fellow tribesmen who succumbed to the lure of liquor. George Suttor once offered Windradyne a glass of rum and water, but he refused to drink it, pointing to his head, which indicated to Suttor that he had had some experience of a hangover!

In 1835 he was badly wounded in a tribal encounter and was taken to the Bathurst Hospital for treatment. Confinement to an institution was too much for this free spirit, and he tore off his bandages and escaped, fleeing to the Suttor property 'Brucedale' where gangrene set in, causing his death There he is buried in the 'Brucedale' tribal cemetery under a plaque reading: The resting place of Windradyne, alias Saturday, the last chief of the aborigines. first a terror, but later a friend to the settlers. Died of wounds received in a tribal encounter 1835. A true patriot.

The Waragery Tribe

Harried we were, and spent,
Broken and falling,
Ere as the cranes we went,
Crying and calling.
Summer shall see the bird
Backward returning,
Never shall there be heard,
Us, who went yearning.
Emptied of us the land;
Ghostly our going;
Fallen, like spears the hand
Dropped in the throwing.
We are the lost who went,
Like the birds, crying;
Hunted, lonely and spent,
Broken and dying.

Mary Gilmore.

Note: In this poem Dame Mary Gilmore used a variant of the usual spelling of Wiradjuri.

6

Henry's Mum

When you come to think of it, life's a bit of a bastard, isn't it?

Take poor old Henry Lawson, one of life's born losers, if ever there was one. In his later years in Sydney people would cross the street if they saw him coming, afraid that he might try to cadge a couple of bob off them to go on another bender. And out in the bush, in towns like Grenfell, where he was born, and Gulgong near Eurunderee, where he went to school, they would not have given him the time of day, though in death they try to share his literary fame by staging Henry Lawson Festivals to entice money-spending tourists to their little backwaters. And as for poor old put-upon mum Louisa Lawson (nee Albury), the REAL achiever of the Lawson family, these days she rarely rates a mention. And the feminists, who owe so much to her pioneering efforts in their cause, sniff with disdain when her name pops up.

For the Lawsons, mother and son, life really was a bastard most of the time.

When 18-year-old Louisa Albury of Eurunderee in 1866 married Peter Hertzberg Larsen, a Norwegian sailor who jumped ship to try his luck on the goldfields, she couldn't have known what she was letting herself in for. The following year, on June 17, Henry was born in a tent on the Grenfell diggings and from that time it was downhill for a long long time until she separated from the unstable Larsen (who by then had anglicised his name to Lawson) and took herself and her four children off to a new life in Sydney - always the 'Big Smoke' to country people like herself. That was around 1883 - the exact date is uncertain.

If you think the single mums of today have it rough, spare a thought for their similarly placed sisters in the 19th Century. No single parent pensions then, few handouts and no back-up social security system of care and benefits of any kind. Widows were treated with some compassion by the (mainly Church) charities, but women who divorced or voluntarily separated from drunken husbands certainly weren't. And doubly frowned on were strongly assertive, militant women in the mould of Louisa Lawson. She really had it tough.

Initially she ran a boarding house, taking any piece work or domestic work offering, while always looking beyond the confines of her drudgery towards distant horizons.

It was Louisa Lawson who discovered that only a small wooden cross marked the grave of Henry Kendall, the poet, in Waverley Cemetery, and who successfully campaigned to raise funds for a proper memorial to be erected over his remains.

It was Louisa Lawson who organised the first Women's Suffrage League in Sydney and who compaigned unceasingly for votes for women.

It was Louisa Lawson who established The Dawn Club, a social reform club for "the advancement and industrial independence of women."

And, of course, it was Louisa Lawson who established and ran for 17 years (1888-1905*) The Dawn*, Australia's first radical feminist magazine. The most remarkable thing about this venture was that it was probably the first long running magazine published anywhere in the world to be produced entirely by women, right through from the editing, composing and machine processes.

This brought Louisa and her all-female team (of up to ten part-time or full time workers) in direct and headlong confrontation with the Typographical Association, the powerful all-male printers' union.

The sustained campaign which the printers waged against *The Dawn* over several years took many forms. First they tried (unsuccessfully) to have it barred from the mails because it was produced by non-union labour. When this failed they instigated a series of boycotts against the magazine, bringing considerable pressure (again unsuccessfully) on its advertisers. When these tactics failed they resorted to a dirty tricks campaign which included noisy demonstrations outside the magazine's office, harassment of the staff (and visitors) coming to and fro, and at one stage holding a large mirror up outside the building so the sun rays would dazzle one of the women carrying a forme of type, hoping that it would cause her to trip and spill the handset type on the floor. And the harassment did not always come from outside, but from quite unexpected quarters in the building. In remarkable interview which appeared in the October 24 1896 issue of *The Bulletin* she related the following story:

" ...and how the men used to come and patronise us, and try to get something out of us!. l remember one day a man from the *Christian World* came round to borrow a (printing) block - a picture. l wouldn't lend it to him; I said we had paid a pound for it, and I couldn't afford to go and buy blocks for other papers. When he stood by the stone and sneered at the girls locking up the formes.

We were just going to press, and you know how locking-up isn't always an easy matter -particularly for new chums like we were.

Well , he stood there and said nasty things, and poor Miss Greig - she's my forewoman - and the girls, they got as white as chalk; the tears were in their eyes. l asked him three times to go, and be wouldn't, so I took up a watering pot full of water that we had for sweeping the floor, and I let him have it.

It went up with a s-swish, and you should have seen him! He was so nicely dressed - all white flannel and straw hat, and spring flowers in his button hole; and it wet him through - knocked his hat off and filled his coat pocket full of water. He was brave, I'll say that; he wouldn't go; he just wiped himself and stood there getting nastier and nastier, and I lost my patience. 'Look here', I said, 'do you know what we do in the bush to tramps that come bothering us? We give them clean water first, and then, if they won't go we give 'em something like this'. And I took up the lye bucket, that we used for cleaning type; it was thick, with an inch of black scum on it like jelly, that wobbled when you shook it. l held it under his nose and said: 'Do you see this!' And he went in a hurry."

Louisa might have been a bit of a battle-axe when it came to fighting men over her rights, but she always claimed that she was not a man-hater. In her eyes women had the rough end of the pineapple in life and had to constantly fight to gain some sort equality. In the same *Bulletin* interview quoted above she put the case succinctly:

"Women are what men make them. Why, a woman can't bear a child without it being received into the hands of a male doctor; it is baptised by a fat old male parson; a girl goes through life obeying laws made by men; and if she breaks them, a male magistrate sends her to gaol where a male warder handles her and locks her in her cell at night to see she's all right.. If she gets so far as to be hanged, a male hangman puts the rope around her neck; she is buried by a male grave-digger; and she goes to Heaven ruled over by a male God or a hell managed by a male devil. isn't it a wonder men didn't make the devil a woman?"

Although it was Henry's poems that always attracted the attention, his mum was also a bit of a dab hand at producing interesting verse, a lot of which appeared in the pages of *The Dawn* over its long existence, or in her only book of poems *The Lonely Crossing and Other Poems* (published 1905). One particular poem 'A Pound A Mile' from this volume, captures the essence of struggles in the bush in the last century as well as any of her son's efforts. It is set in a bush shearing shed and tells of the agony of the top gun shearer, whose wife is in a tent nearby almost certainly near to death in a very difficult child birth. Asked why he hasn't called the doctor, he explains to his mates that he hasn't any money and that Dr Pile in the nearest town, sixty-five miles away, charges a pound a mile to go out of town.

In typical mateship of the bush fashion, the men (and the boss) rally around, passing the hat to collect the money for the doctor, and in the wee small hours the doctor gets through, the blood mare in the sulky:

"limping came
all tucked and blown. and wet and white.
And panting hard, but game".

And as becomes all good stories, there is a happy ending with the doctor saving both mother and babe:

"Thank God", he said, "My work is done".
As Tommy's hand he pressed;
"I've saved your wife and little son,
Let Nature do the rest".

And then they went into the shed -
The men and Dr Pile -
And drank his health in Queensland red,
And paid him - pound for mile.

But best of all I like the short poem called 'The Reformers' which seems to sum up life and aspirations of Louisa Lawson and the many other often long-forgotten pioneers of the women's reform movement:

We lead the way, we lead the way,
We rise alert to meet each day,
We start the fight, we head the fray,
We lead the way, we lead the way.
We turn the sod, we stir the pool,
We point the way to those who rule,
We check the rogue, we chide the fool,
We point the way to those who rule.
We bear reverse, we breast rebuff,
We force a way o'er passes rough
We stand the kick, we take the cuff.
Till Death's stern umpire calls "Enough".

7

Remittance Men

A much neglected field of study in Australian history is the legion of English remittance men who in the 19th Century were shunted off to the colonies of the British Empire because of having transgressed the laws our outstayed their welcome in family circles.

Some were hastily bundled out of the Old Dart to prevent them having to face up to some criminal charge in court, thus bringing disgrace to some illustrious family name; others simply threatened the family fortune because of their gambling habits. In such instance the family concerned considered the best solution to the problem was to exile the offending member to some far off destination with a small but regular stipend on the understanding he would assume a different name in this new clime and never again darken the doors of the family home. Out of sight, out of mind, was the slogan for the times.

Nobody knows how many miscreants were shipped abroad in the colonial period under this little acknowledged system, since the families in the Old Country maintained a tight-lipped silence on the subject of the family Black Sheep. The Remittance Men, as they came to be known - there seems to have been no female Remittance Women involved - simply took a new name in their adopted land and tried to put the unhappy past behind them. An appreciable number seemed to have spent their monthly remittances on grog and drank themselves into early graves. However, quite a few turned over a new leaf and gave up the drink or gambling or whatever demon had been possessing them - at least for a while. Some even made good in a big way and became very useful citizens in their new domicile. It is worth pursuing the careers of a couple of these remittance men, one who made good permanently and another who had an unhappy lapse.

In this latter category was Australia's most famous 19th Century remittance man, Sir Frederick William Pottinger, Bart., who, if he didn't achieve fame in real life was immortalised in literature as "Sir Ferdinand Morringer" in Rolf Boldrewood's great adventure story *Robbery Under Arms*.

Sir Frederick was born in 1831, in India, the second son of Sir Henry Pottinger, Bart., a distinguished soldier and diplomat, who had long served in the East India Company, and who traced his lineage back to Egbert. After his service in the East India Company he achieved distinction in the diplomatic service in India and as the first Governor of Hong Kong, and Governor of the Cape of Good Hope and later Madras.

With such a background it is not surprising that Sir Frederick's early life embraced both Eton and the Grenadier Guards. The young man was commissioned as lieutenant in the 2nd Battalion of the Grenadier Guards in 1850 but as his regiment was at that time not serving abroad his actual military experience was nil. His knowledge of the race track, the opera, the gambling halls and other early delights of London however, was extensive. Living with his mother, Lady Pottinger, who adored him and catered to his every whim, he led a bohemian life of extreme abandon. He gambled so heavily on the racetrack that Lady Pottinger was forced to sell her jewels to pay for his debts, and Frederick was forced to sell his lieutenant's commission and quit the Guards in 1854.

His dissolute ways lead to a serious breach with his father, but before things could come to a head Sir Henry died in March 1856. As Sir Henry's first born son had died in infancy, Frederick inherited both the title and the greater portion of his father's wealth. The new Sir Frederick continued on his merry, profligate ways dissipating his fortune of more than a hundred thousand pounds in record time. As he was still up to his eyes in gambling debts, the remaining family members decided that it would be for the good of England, and the family if Frederick were to disappear forever to the Antipodes.

It is believed that Sir Frederick came to Australia late in 1856, the same year he inherited his title and blew his huge inheritance. In the colony he adopted the name of Parker and headed for the goldfields in search of wealth undergound. Being unsuccessful in this search, he joined the New South Wales Police Force as a mounted trooper and appears to have spent the next few years as a trooper running the gold escorts on the western fields.

His true identity became known to the authorities when a letter from England arrived at Police Headquarters addressed to Sir Frederick William Pottinger. Having identified their lowly ranked trooper as a Knight of the Realm, the authorities were in a bit of a bind. It was hardly infra dig to have a full flown hereditary Knight galloping around the countryside or directing traffic in Pitt Street! They were staunchly loyalist and royalist times when tugging the forelock was widely practised at all levels.

The authorities looked around for a posting more in keeping with Sir Frederick's station in life. The only post open at the time was in my home town of Dubbo. So that is how in November 1860, Sir Frederick Pottinger came to Dubbo as Clerk of Petty Sessions and District Registrar of Births, Deaths and Marriages. Dubbo therefore had the distinction of being the only town in the world - then or since - to have enjoyed the privilege of having a Baronet as its Clerk of Petty Sessions.

No records survive of his life in Dubbo but his duties cannot have been too arduous as *Bell's Life in Sydney*, was later to comment on this period in Sir Frederick's life ".... he was fond of writing, and to kill the. monotony of his Dubbo life, was in the habit of writing for a Bathurst and local journal. Some gems of poetry under the sobriquet 'Wussa Australians' may be familiar to some readers."

Sir Frederick remained in Dubbo for eleven months, until October 1861 when he was appointed Assistant Superintendent of the Southern Mounted Patrol and Gold Escorts on a salary of two hundred and seventy five pounds a year. The following month he was also appointed a Magistrate.

In his new role he was stationed at Burrangong, where he had earlier served as a trooper. He had been in town only a month when he was involved in a billiard room incident at a hotel. He struck a man named Thomas Watt with a billiard cue, forcing his head through a window. Watt sued Pottinger for two hundred pounds for assault. He won his case but the jury awarded Watt only a shilling in damages.

Reporting the event, the *Yass Courier* noted that at the time of the incident (well after midnight when the pot-house by law should have been closed) Sir Frederick as the chief police officer and a magistrate, should have been setting an example to the community instead of being embroiled in "not over-creditable conflict with a butcher".

It was an incident that should have brought the instant dismissal of Sir Frederick, but the NSW Premier Charles Cowper, who was also the Colonial Secretary, decided to thrash his errant knight with a feather. Cowper issued a public statement, saying that Sir Frederick's behaviour had been "highly discreditable" and urging officers to be more circumspect. It was a long-winded missive full of homilies and motherhood statements, all of which Sir Frederick was instructed to circulate to all other NSW Superintendents. And there the matter was allowed to rest despite strong criticism being directed at the Premier in the Legislative Assembly for his handling the matter. One member summed it up rather neatly when he said that Pottinger's title seemed to have "exercised a mesmeric influence" on the Premier.

On February 10 1862 Sir Frederick was transferred to the Lachlan district and instructed to hunt down bushrangers which at that time were becoming both numerous and troublesome in most southern New South Wales areas. The most notorious of these brigands was Frank Gardiner who led Sir Frederick and his men on many a wild goose chase around the southern countryside in the next few years. Time and time, Gardiner was able to slip through nets cast by Sir Frederick, mainly due to the incompetence of the poorly equipped and poorly paid troopers he had under his command. Nor was he helped by the vast territory under his control and the fact that Gardener, Ben Hall and other bushrangers could count on a great deal of support from various settlers.

Both Sydney newspapers and the country press were highly critical of Sir Frederick, but many of the attacks were not based on solid evidence or were political in bias, being aimed at the government of the day rather than Pottinger. In some ways Sir Frederick Pottinger was a victim of the good old Tall Poppy syndrome and perhaps he would not have attracted nearly so much flak if he had not had a title, an upper crust English accent and a definite way with the ladies!

In the end Sir Frederick became a political liability to the government and when he breached Police Regulations in January 1865 by twice riding horses in the Wowingragong Races he was summarily sacked.

While the Sydney press generally supported the action of the government, out in the bush there was strong support for Sir Frederick and a large number of protest meetings were quickly organised and petitions were circulated calling for his reinstatement.

Given the tide of sentiment in Sir Frederick's favour in the districts where he had served, the Government might well have had a change of heart, especially as they had "hung him on a fairly slender thread of misdoing", but they didn't get a chance to review the matter.

Buoyed by the support he was receiving, Sir Frederick packed his bags to go to Sydney to plead his case. But he never made it. In March 1865 at a coach stop at Wascoe's Inn in the Blue Mountains, between Hartley and Penrith, Sir Frederick wandered into an orchard adjoining the hotel to pick some fruit. He dallied too long at the task and the coach set off without him. He ran after it and swinging himself aboad the pistol in his pocket accidentally discharged and wounded him in the abdomen. His wound proved more serious than first thought and he died on April 9, aged 34.

During his years in the NSW Police Force he had never managed to conquer the drinking and gambling problems that were the cause of his undoing in England. In all the colonial years he was dependent on the regular family "remittances" in addition to the fairly substantial amounts (for the times) he was paid as a senior police officer. But for all that he was probably more sinned against than sinner, and perhaps the last word on this our most distinguished, remittance man, should go to the anonymous editorial writer in *The Burrangong Argus* who penned these words in his memory in the paper's issue of April 15 1865: " ...His British rank and his colonial position afforded a a never-failing theme for the spiteful comments of narrow-minded men, ever eager to drag one socially superior down to their own level. The men who were under him never joined in this senseless howl; they saw him as he was, and were aware of the injustice of the clamour raised against him."

While Sir Frederick Pottinger may have failed the reform test in his adopted land, there were other remittance men who turned over a new leaf (permanently) in the Antipodes and went on to found successful enterprises and to sire a host of noted Australians. And amongst these was John Robinson, though it is unlikely the average reader of these chronicles would have heard of him. So here you are reading a "first", the story of a successful remittance man.

John Robinson was born in York, England, in 1788 to a well connected family, his first cousin being the Marquess of Ripon. His surviving descendants do not know what misdeeds caused him to attract the title of 'Black Sheep' of the family in England, or why or when they shipped him off to Australia as a remittance man. All they know is that some time in the early years of the last century he was located in Van Diemens Land where he met and married Ann Wade, who had a fascinating history of her own. She was the daughter of Catherine Morgan, born on Norfolk Island in 1792 to a First Fleet convict, Richard Morgan and Second Fleet convict, Catherine Clarke.

Catherine Morgan in 1806 married John Wade (or Wayde) who was born in England in 1775 and became the first Sheriff of Van Diemens Land. Their only child, Ann Wade, was born in 1808 and on August 23 1824, at the age of 16, she married John Robinson, who was then 36. Their first child, Isaac Robinson, was born at Macquarie Plains, Van Diemens Land, on June 28 1825, and it is he who is the main subject of this story, since his life was an unusual one, to say the least.

Little is known of his early life but around 1864 he visited Norfolk Island (where his grandmother had been born a half century earlier) as a crew member of an American whaler. He tarried a while on the island and rather indiscreetly got not one but two Quintal girls pregnant. The elder girl, Kezia, was 21 at the time and her sister Hannah was 16. The girls had a discussion on the situation and it was decided that Hannah, being the younger and in more need of support, should marry Isaac.

Family legend has it that Isaac, who was then 40, was a reluctant bridegroom as he didn't fancy spending the rest of his life on an island. He decided to make a bolt for it but a boatload of irate male Quintals, all descendants of the Pitcairn Island Bounty mutineers, decided otherwise, so Isaac was forced to face up to his filial duties. He and Hannah were married on June 12 1865, the ceremony being conducted by the Bishop of Melanesia, who happened to be visiting Norfolk Island at the time.

The marriage was a fruitful one as the couple had eleven children, of whom four died at birth or in early infancy. Their first born was a son John Dunsmere Robinson, born late in 1875, while Kezia produced a daughter, Sarah Alice Robinson. Kezia died three years later (in 1788) while Sarah Alice died in 1881. Only one of the Robinson children directly concern our story, and that is Enoch Cobcroft ("Cobby") Robinson born on November 5 1875.

After his marriage to Hannah, Isaac settled down to life on the island, and they lived in a cottage at Kingston, while Isaac conducted a farm at Steele's Point, supplying vegetables and cattle to the Melanesian Mission. Their cottage at Kingston incidentally, was renovated and restored in 1968, being the only surviving wooden structure built on the island during the Second Penal Settlement of 1825-1856.

But Isaac's interests extended far beyond tilling the soil and raising cattle. He was probably better educated than anyone else on the island in this period and this enabled him to play a leading role in Island affairs. At various times he was the Secretary of the Council of Elders, Clerk of the Court and Registrar of Births, Deaths and Marriages and correspondent for the *Sydney Morning Herald* and for New Zealand newspapers.

But his greatest abiding interest was in the field of botany He was for many years active in the island's Horticultural Society and corresponded with and collected island specimens for Baron von Mueller. His diaries are replete with long and learned botanical names and dissertations on the plant life of the island. He discovered a new species of fern and had it correctly classified. It is known as *Robinsoni*.

Perhaps his most unusual post was as the only United States of America Consul for Norfolk Island. No doubt this came about as result of some early experience with the whaling industry, which in the last century played a large role in the island's economy. Many American whaling ships made regular calls at the island to process their hauls, and quite a few American whalers are the buried on the island. All this must have persuaded Americans that it would be in their interests to have a Consul on the Island, so Isaac Robinson was appointed to that post on November 18 1887, the agency being accountable to the Sydney US Consulate. He was the only appointee to the post as the agency was closed on July 1 1908.

A photo of Isaac taken in 1902, shows him as being bald with a short neat beard, looking much younger than his 77 years. Another decade down the track he started seriously thinking about his family connections back in England. The Marquess of Ripon had died without heirs, but Isaac's father, John Robinson, had died back in 1859. When no claimant turned up in England, the title and its lands reverted to the Crown. Isaac felt he might have some claim to the title, if not to the lands, so in 1912 he set sail for England with intent of laying claim to the old title. But he never did make it as he took ill and died on the voyage between Norfolk Island and Sydney and was buried at sea on November 19 1912, at the grand old age of 87. Hannah, his wife of 47 years, died two years later on August 24 1914.

Isaac Robinson's life was a long and fruitful one, and along the way he produced a large brood of young Robinsons whose descendants seem to be interlinked with the whole history of Norfolk Island as well as Pitcairn Island and the Mutiny on the Bounty, including the Buffets, the Ouintals, the Adams, the Christians, and even that remarkable adventurer George Hunn Nobbs, the illegitimate son of Jemima Ffrench and Francis Rawdon Hastings, the Marquess of Hastings and Earl of Moira. Hobbs arrived on Pitcairn island in 1828, imposed himself on the islanders and acted as a benevolent pastor/dictator to an acquiescent flock of islanders for the next 55 years! And on his mother's side Isaac had a whole batch of relatives prominent in Australian show business, numbering all the talented Lamonds, as well as Toni Lamond's sister, Helen Reddy.

Remember his son "Cobby" Robinson. He too has left his mark on the life and history of Norfolk Island. On April 20 1899 he married a distant cousin, Jemima Louisa Quintal, the famous "Aunt Jemima", so well known to so many visitors to the island before her death in 1970. Their son Graham Robinson (later renamed

Graham Ion-Robinson) was the grandfather of a very well known and distinguished member of the present day hierarchy of Norfolk Island, Cedric Newton Ion-Robinson, better known to everyone simply as Ric Robinson.

In recent years Ric Robinson, when he was Deputy President of the Island's Legislative Assembly and Minister for Commerce and Environment, led the fight to secure more independence for the islanders who want to determine their own destiny free from the many shackles presently imposed by Canberra.

And backing him up in this campaign, which at times promised to rival in intensity the original Mutiny on the Bounty, was his wife Colleen McCullough, even better known to the world at large as Australia's richest novelist (*The Thorn Birds* etc.).

Perhaps when Colleen has at last finished her researches on the Roman Empire, and the lives of Caesar, Cicero and Brutus, she may turn her attention to an epic closer to home, namely her husband's remarkable family, going back in one direction to the Bounty Mutiny and in another to a distinguished Remittance Man.

Old Isaac Robinson, Ric's great great grandfather, alone should be worth a volume in such an epic tale, as he kept diaries over thirty years, most of which survive in Ric's possession, and these are supplemented by plenty of family documents including Isaac letting off considerable steam about five pounds owing to him for postage by the parsimonious American Consul in Sydney.

And it is tempting to speculate on how different Norfolk Island history would have been had Kezia and Hannah Quintal had some basic knowledge of contraception, or an inclination to say "No" to Isaac; or if the Quintal lads had been slower off the mark in launching their longboat, thus enabling Isaac to escape to England, perhaps to become the new Marquess of Ripon!

8

A Letter from Elizabeth

If you take any year of Australian history in the century after white settlement in 1788 you will find it like a giant jig saw puzzle with fragments of historical events and lives of people aplenty, but gaps everywhere. For some years the gaps are very numerous and significant, for other periods less so.

Occasionally historical fossickers will come across a missing piece in one of these jig saws in the shape of a document or previously unrecorded letter that sheds a little extra light on the period of its origin.

The recent discovery of a previously unrecorded letter of 1836, written from Camden Park by Elizabeth, the eldest maiden daughter of John Macarthur, fills in a few interesting pieces in the jig saw pattern of that year.

To put these pieces into their proper perspective it is necessary to take into account the Macarthur family fortunes at that time.

Four years earlier, in 1832, the mental illness that had plagued John Macarthur most of his adult life, came to a head and he was removed from the Legislative Council at the request of Governor

Bourke on the grounds that he had been "pronounced a lunatic... with little hope of his restoration". Two years on he died, on April 11 1834, and was buried quietly at Camden Park, the great family estate which was home for Macarthurs for so long.

After his illness the running of Camden Park was taken over jointly by his son William and his eldest daughter Elizabeth, his eldest son James being engaged elsewhere in political matters.

And when Elizabeth sat down to start her long letter some time in December 1836 (it was written over several weeks, there being no great hurry since she mentioned that it would be carried to England on one of the wool ships "which will be sailing in January or February"), William was also away from Camden Park on some business so she was in charge to the estate.

Elizabeth was then 44, a spinster, and in failing health (she was to die two years later), but this wasn't always so. Many years earlier when she was in the full bloom of her womanhood, a suitor had come a-wooing. And a very eligible suitor at that, no less than the formidable William Charles Wentworth. What a union of the two most prominent colonial families that would have been. But, alas, a quarrel developed between the young Wentworth and her father, over a loan, one to the other, and both being of fiery temperament and stubborn nature, the dispute quickly developed into a feud and the young Wentworth was proclaimed persona non gratia at Camden Park, putting a quick end to the budding romance.

Elizabeth's letter was addressed to Mrs Colonel Erskine, of Weymouth, England, and was a long and chatty epistle, mainly to do with family matters and the entwined business interests of the Macarthurs and Erskines since the latter owned Erskine Park at Melville, adjoining Camden Park. In the absence of the Erskines, then living in retirement in England, the Macarthurs acted as their agents in the matter of Erskine Park, supervising the running of the property and preparing it for an early sale.

Erskine Park was a showcase estate, comprising 3000 acres and built up from a land grant acquired in the early years of the colony by James Erskine (1765-1825) soldier, and Lieutenant Governor of New South Wales from 1817. In 1819 he was promoted to Colonel and in February 1823 he returned to England. In 1825 he was posted to India but died of cholera four days after reaching Madras. His eldest son, also a Colonel, inherited , being an absentee landlord of the Erskine Estate, with the Macarthurs overseers with a Power of Attorney.

Elizabeth in her letter to Mrs Erskine gave a running account of current market conditions and expressed the opinion that the time was fast approaching to consider putting the property on the market, since trading conditions in the colony were improving. She recommended selling the cattle by auction and the property separately. The property at that time was being leased by a Mr Bayman.

The Erskine's son, Lieutenant Erskine, had only recently been posted to the colony and Elizabeth mentioned that she had been introduced to him a few days earlier. She went on to say that he was in perfect health "having recently returned from an expedition to the Hunter River, one of the northern districts, where the aboriginal natives have been committing some outrages". Elizabeth said the young man's Colonel (whose name I cannot decipher) had informed her that the young Lieutenant "had discharged his duty much to his satisfaction."

What Elizabeth is saying in the double-speak language of the period, was that Lieutenant Erskine had led a party up to the Hunter Valley and shot every aboriginal they could find before returning safely to Sydney Town.

Here we have here is an independent report of a previously

unrecorded massacre of aborigines in December 1836. Another tiny piece of the jig saw falling into its slot. But how many other similar pieces still remain to be unearthed to give us further glimpses of the Hidden History of our blood soaked continent?

9

A Yank Down Under

Next time you meet up with an American ask him/her this question: Name the only President of the United States who lived and worked in Australia?

When this draws only blank looks or wrong answers, as it usually will, provide a clue, that the gentleman concerned had at the time a rather passionate affair with an Australian barmaid! From personal experience I can guarantee this question, even with the provocative clue thrown in, will completely toss most Americans, even those fairly well up on their nation's history. And it will also toss most Australians too because the individual's name is conspicuously absent from most Australian histories despite the considerable influence, usually far from benign, he exerted over our affairs for more than a decade.

The answer to my question is Herbert Hoover, President of the USA from 1929-1933, a fraudulent trickster, a conman of considerable talents and probably the most corrupt President to have occupied the White House. No mean achievement!

Herbert Clark Hoover was born on August 10 1874, in the

village of West Branch, Iowa, where his father, Jessie Hoover, was the village blacksmith. The strict Quaker family was of German stock having descended from Andreas Huber, who anglicised his name after migrating to North Carolina around 1740.

Jessie Hoover died when the lad was six, and he was orphaned three years later when his mother also died. For two years he was shuttled around farms of the Hoover family. When he was eleven his mother's brother, his uncle John Minthorn, appeared on the scene and carried him off to his home at Newberg on the west coast of Oregon.

Uncle John was a pious old fraud, a snake oil salesman, who hid his unsavoury dealing in sub-divided swamp lands behind a phony mask of being a lay preacher and a medical man, calling himself Dr Minthorn when the need arose. He also ran a small private school where his nephew Herbert was expected to do the cleaning and odd jobs in between picking up snippets of education. In his teens he helped his Uncle out with various chores at the office of the Oregon Land Company, no doubt acquiring many dubious tricks of that trade which he was able to put into practice in later life with considerable effect.

When Herbert was 17 his Uncle's misdeeds caught up with him and the Oregon Land Co came crashing down about his ears. Two things then conspired to send young Herbert careering off in a new direction.

The first was when a visiting speaker came through Newberg proclaiming that geology was the career of the future. About this time the Leland Stanford Junior University was struggling to get established at nearby Paolo Alto. At that stage it was little more than a private Senior High School, bearing no resemblance to the great institution it would later become. And it was seeking to enrol students for its initial courses, including geology.

Herbert's education had been rudimentary to say the least and there was no way he could have passed any normal entrance exam. But Stanford was just starting up and needed a student body desperately. They weren't fussy about standards and enrolled Herbert for their four year geology course. There were no student fees but there was a charge of twenty dollars a month for board and lodging and Herbert earned this by working in the laundry of the college.

Fellow students described Herbert Hoover as a loner who had no friends and who did not participate in sports or social activities of the college. But he was genuinely interested in the course subject, seemed to have a flair for mathematics and managed to cope except in English, where he invariably failed. As the College couldn't afford any failures among the seven students in the geology course the college had one of the staff, "Professor" JP Smith, prepare Hoover's English papers.

As a result in 1895 all seven geology students graduated and were given Diplomas stating they had completed a four year course in geology. This was the only piece of academic paper Herbert Hoover ever acquired but he used it to such good purpose that he was able to bluff his way through life thereafter as an expert Mining Engineer.

But such pieces of paper had no current value in the job market of the time, so Hoover spent the next year drifting around various western mining camps, picking up bits and pieces of knowledge where he could and accepting any odd jobs on offer. His longest stint was at the Mayflower Mine in Nevada where he worked for two months as a trimmer, an underground labourer hauling trolleys at two dollars fifty an hour.

At the beginning of 1896 he was back on the west coast and landed a job as a junior clerk in the San Francisco office of Louis

Janin, a Belgian who operated as a mining engineer consultant. The pay was thirty dollars a month, barely enough for subsistence even back in those low cost days. Then a new opportunity opened up out of the blue when Janin received a request from a London firm it represented, asking him to find an experienced mining engineer, single, aged about 35, prepared to go to the Western Australian goldfields to do survey work at a salary of three thousand dollars a year.

Janin had no way of finding an experienced engineer prepared to go to far off Australia for that sort of money. He decided that Hoover looked much older than his 22 years and might just pass for 35 years. Providing credentials was certainly a problem but Janin, who appears to have had few ethics, worked on it with Hoover and came up with a completely fictitious record covering seven years and reading:

Graduate in Mining, Stanford University, USA; one year **Geologist**, Geological Survey, Arkansas (lead and zinc investigation); two and a half years Geologist, US Geological Survey (gold and silver); one year **Surveyor**, **Assayer**, **Foreman** and **Superintendent** at Grass Valley, Nevada City, Angelo Camp, California and Clifton, Arizona etc.; three years mostly **Chief Assistant to Louis Janin** making the usual examinations all over the Western USA. **In charge at New Mexico** and **Four Mile, Colorado.**

Armed with this imposing but totally phoney resume, Herbert Hoover sailed to London to present himself to his prospective new employers, Bewick Moreing & Company. And here it is necessary to provide some background.

When large scale gold deposits were discovered in Western Australia in the early 1890's it sparked a stampede to the new fields by thousands in their rush to be rich, for as Virgil noted: "Cursed craze for gold, how thou dost affect the minds of men!" There were two ways of getting rich at that time: The hard way of going to the fields and physically digging up the yellow stuff - the path followed by the multitude. The other way, the easy way, was to sit behind a desk in far off London and create on paper prospectuses that would cause countless fools to part with large sums of money for shares in worthless mines on the other side of the world.

There were many small practitioners of this dubious art, but three main players stood out head and shoulders above the herd. The earliest major player amongst the share manipulators was Whitaker Walker, an exceedingly smart operator who came unstuck when he ventured into outside ventures such as the Bakerloo Line on the London Underground. He crashed in 1903, fled to the USA with one of his mistresses, but was extradited back to face twenty six counts of fraud. Found guilty and sentenced to seven years gaol, he promptly swallowed a cyanide pill and expired on the spot. Exit number one.

The second big player was Horatio Bottomley who was aged 33 and a bankrupt when the Western Australian gold rush started. He made a deal with his creditors and rose Lazarus-like from the ashes to float a whole string of worthless mines over the next two decades. He became a member of Parliament, founded the newspaper *John Bull* and was not nailed by the law until 1923 when he was gaoled for three years on various counts of fraud. He died ten years later, a pauper, kept alive in his declining years by the generosity of a former mistress. At least he had a good run for his money, even if his numerous victims didn't.

The third, and most important player in this nest of top drawer swindlers, was Charles Algernon Moreing, who was firmly in control of Bewick Moreing & Company when Herbert Hoover arrived in London early in 1897 to present his credentials.

The company had been established back in 1865 by Thomas Bewick, a widely respected coal mining figure, whose brother was the Bishop of Newcastle. Bewick made the move in forming Bewick & Co late in life to provide some kind of tenure for his reclusive son, Thomas Burrell Bewick. Within a few years it became apparent that Bewick junior was quite incapable of running the business of mining consultants, so Bewick senior brought in a promising Pupil (apprentice) Charles Moreing, and the firm was renamed Bewick Moreing & Company. When Bewick senior died, Moreing assumed total control and changed direction in a manner that must have had the old man spinning in his grave.

With Bewick senior gone, the firm had no mining experience or qualifications to draw on. But this did not deter Moreing one whit in promoting his firm as mining experts.

In those days the "salting" of a mine prior to its sale was a common enough practice but Moreing used more sophisticated techniques. He purchased or obtained an option on a mine, floated a company with dubious claims based on very "iffy" reports supplied by the compliant managers appointed in charge. His firm acted as managers for this newly launched mine and the by-laws contained waiver clauses with options. If the mine showed promise he and his insiders exercised the options and gained complete control of the operation. If the mine was a "dud" (as nine out of ten were) he simply creamed off all capital raised through exorbitant management fees and the punters were left lamenting when the mine was abandoned, thus proving Mark Twain's contention that a mine was a hole in the ground with with a liar on top! It was also a case of Heads I win, Tails you lose for Moreing who was in a no risk situation as his outlays were minimal.

When Herbert Hoover, at 22 claiming to be 35 and with a wildly faked resume, landed on his doorstep Moreing must have smelt a large sized rat because inflated claims were part and parcel of the English mining scene at the time. As Carton Booth put it in *Another England*, when writing of the period:

"To be a nephew or some distant relative of one who had at some time in his life been a 'mining captain' in Cornwall, was quite enough to constitute a man a mining surveyor; whilst a stock of impudence and an engagement in a blacksmith's shop for six months was sufficient to set a 'mining engineer' up in trade. "

If Moreing had any doubts he kept them to himself, heeding the words of Horace: "Greed and money first - and all the rest after". In fact, Hoover's obvious duplicity might well have been a point in the young man's favour. After all the main thing that Moreing was seeking was a compliant surveyor on the goldfields, so Hoover was dispatched immediately, arriving on Australian soil (at Albany) for the first time on March 13 1897.

His brief was to look over the existing Bewick Moreing mines and to seek out possible prospects for acquisition. Whether by foresight or sheer luck, Bewick Moreing & Company had in their stable the original Hannan's Brownhill mine, which only then was starting to reveal its potential, and which in time was to prove a bonanza for its shareholders, enabling Moreing to use it as a "milk cow" to prop up returns from the many duds on the company list. During his initial stay of 18 months on the goldfields Hoover produced only one "find", the Sons of Gwalior mine, which he thought had possibilities. He recommended its acquisition and his judgment proved right in the long run, though initial work in the six months he was in charge of the mine as manager was disappointing. This spell however, had one side benefit of revealing how tough he could be under pressure. The miners' unions were making strong demand which Hoover refused to meet. He met them head-on by importing Italians under contracts that were extremely onerous (to the workers). When other mines saw how successful Hoover had been in this respect, they too took on the unions, resulting in considerable upheaval on the fields,

After 18 months Moreing recalled Hoover to England as he had a much more important assignment for him in China. Moreing had his eye on the Kaiping coal mine (said to be the world's largest) in Tientsin. This privately owned mine had huge deposits of coal which were being mined uneconomically by thousands of low paid coolies without the benefit of any mechanisation. The Chinese government was known to be anxious to step up production to earn more export dollars.

Moreing had secured for Hoover a position at the mine as a "Mining Expert" at the very respectable salary of $15,000 per year. Ostensibly his job was to advise the owners how they could mechanise the mine and increase efficiency. His REAL mission was as an on-the-spot spy for Moreing to work out a scheme for the total "reconstruction" of the mine's ownership so that it all ended up in the control of Berwick Moreing & Company. The deal had the secret blessing of the British Foreign Office (ie. the government) because control of the mine would enable the British to gain a firm foothold in the strategic ice-free harbour of Ching Wan Tao, only sixty miles by rail from the mines.

Despite the inconvenient outbreak of the Boxer Rebellion, Hoover managed to negotiate an agreement along the lines sought by Moreing, whereby the vast properties of the Chinese Engineering and Mining Company Limited, would be amalgamated with a new company to be formed in London by Berwick Moreing & Company. Under what looked like a cosy arrangement on paper, the Chinese retained working control of the new operation with vast injections of capital, machinery and expertise to be provided by new foreign shareholders. Of course, like all of Moreing's schemes nothing was so simple and the Chinese were taken for the proverbial hayride.

A key to the whole contract was a Deed of Trust which had to be executed in China before the scheme went ahead. It was here that Hoover executed his great masterpiece. The Deed of Trust was supposed to have been executed in the name of Bewick Moreing & Company but when it came to the signing, Hoover inserted his own name on the document, blandly explaining that the deed had to be executed in China and that as he was Bewick Moreing & Company's authorised agent it would have to be in his name. The Chinese attorney fell for this three card trick and the deed was executed.

When Hoover turned up in London bearing the deed in his name, Moreing was furious at being double-crossed by his employee in this way. But Hoover was holding all the trump cards. Without him the lucrative deal could not proceed. His demands were a share of the profits and partnership in Bewick Moreing & Co. Moreing had no choice but bow to the inevitable and Bewick junior having long since departed the firm became Moreing Hoover & Company.

The new company was formed and, as was inevitable, the Chinese were taken to the cleaners. Hoover's initial "take" for setting up the deal was estimated at half a million dollars - a fortune in 1901 - and this set him up on his long career of money making by dubious methods.

Meanwhile it was two years before the Chinese discovered how they had been duped and the first reaction of the Government was to have the Empress strip the chief Chinese negotiator, Mandarin Chang Yen Mao, of all honours and titles. Chang was then ordered to recover the lost mines and the port of Ching Wan Tao for the Chinese under penalty of losing his head.

The unhappy Chang decided they did not have the military power to take the mines and port by force. So he went to England and engaged lawyers to take action in the English courts to force the issue. The London lawyers involved were placed in a very awkward position knowing from private talks with the Home Office that there was no way the British were going to haul down the flag either from the mines or the port. As a consequence they felt they could not present a claim for return of the properties on the grounds that fraud had been committed. They reached a compromise with Chang that the Chinese would only claim enforcement of the Memorandum Agreement which Hoover and Chang had signed on February 19 1901.

As is usual in such cases, the matter dragged on in the courts for several years, with lawyers for Moreing Hoover & Co offering every legal obstruction available to them. Finally, on March 1 1905 Mr Justice Joyce in the High Court Chancery Division brought down a verdict in favour of the Chinese, with costs taxed against the Defendants, and Mandarin Chang was able to return to China with his head intact and to have his former titles restored to him. But it was only a half victory for the Chinese who did not succeed in getting back full control of the mines until after the Sun Yat Sen revolution of 1911.

Meanwhile Herbert Hoover was definitely *non persona gratia* in China so had to look elsewhere to pursue his career. It was decided by Moreing that Hoover should take over the Australian operations where there were signs of further potential.

In the years 1901-4 Hoover made a number of lengthy visits to Australia, usually of two or three months duration, and in 1905 he appears to have returned to live, staying until 1907 when he was called away to attend to more important interests of the firm in other parts of the globe.

It is difficult to pinpoint his activities in this period, but Herbert Barker, author of *Camels and the Outback*, does throw light on one unusual endeavour by Hoover which he claims started around 1903. This was when Hoover brought from France a Panhard motor car to get around the various Western Australian mines under his control. This initial import was such a success, reports Barker, that Hoover was able to make an unheard of journey of 125 miles in a single day. This prompted him to import three more of the cars for company use, making it probably the largest commercial fleet of cars then operating in Australia. Of course, Hoover had a big advantage over single car owners since each of his mines had a workshop attached so they were in a good position to make running repairs if a car broke down on any sector of the goldfields. Barker also records that Hoover's small fleet primarily used the tracks originally laid down by the camel drivers and in recognition of this fact he paid a tribute to the camel teams for allowing him to use the tracks.

Hoover's activities in Australia in this period are not nearly so well documented as his shorter stay in the 1890's, but they must have been considerable because in 1905 thirty two Australian mines were listed under the management or control of Moreing Hoover & Company. These interests extended beyond the Western Australian goldfields, which always remained the company's base, to interests in a zinc mine at Broken Hill and an operation at Mt Isa. It can be safely assumed that the main beneficiaries of these operations were always Moreing and Hoover, not the unlucky shareholders who put up the money in the first place. Hoover, as well as Moreing, seemed to have a very cavalier attitude towards the money other people entrusted to him. Back in London in 1908 he became embroiled in a controversy with some irate shareholders who complained that the eight hundred thousand pounds they had subscribed to a Moreing Hoover managed company for a specific purpose had been spent in a different manner and apparently had been "lost or mislaid" somewhere.

Hoover ultimately responded to this complaint by writing as follows in the *Mining Magazine* (London) of May 1912:

"Capital raised is not always spent on the original purpose but is often invested in more reproductive (sic) purpose than if it had remained in the hands of the idiots who parted with it."

There is an old Yankee saying that the man who steals a nickel is a thief, but a man who steals a million dollars is a genius. On this basis both Moreing and Hoover would have to qualify for recognition as being of Super Genius Status. How they achieved this distinction is perhaps best summed up by Sir George Lewin, the very eminent British Counsel who represented them in the Chinese case and other cases in which the pair were involved. Writing in his memoirs after his retirement in 1911 he wrote:

"Many of the huge fortunes which have been amassed by mushroom 'financiers' and promoters during the past decade have been built up on the foundations of trickery, deceit and fraud, and if we examine the methods employed we find them little different to those of the racecourse Thimble Rigger".

And Sir George, perhaps better than anyone else was in a position to pass judgment in his matter.

The peace time activities of Moreing Hoover & Company were given an enormous boost by the outbreak of World War I in 1914 since they had interests of one kind or another in mines all over the place. The price of minerals of all kinds skyrocketed daily adding mightily to their already extensive coffers. And Hoover quickly seized the opportunity to add a profitable little sideline to his many activities when Germany invaded Belgium. Soon the newspapers of the Allied countries were filled with headline stories (largely untrue) of starving Belgian women and children under the cruel yoke of the Hunnish occupation.

To rectify this a Commission for the Relief of Belgium was set up (with committees in all the Allied countries) to send food, medical supplies and other humanitarian aid to the downtrodden Belgians, to be channelled through the neutral countries. And Chief Executive Officer of the Commission was Herbert Clark Hoover.

The response around the world to the appeal for aid for the Belgians was enormous. Even the tiny population of far-off Australia responded by collecting and sending two and a half million dollars. A lot of this, of course, was naturally absorbed by "administrative costs" but such was the flood of donations that millions were left over to purchase the goods. These were purchased by the Commission at inflated prices and surprisingly a lot did actually get through to Belgium by various routes, with permission of the Germans. But none of it was actually **given** to the needy Belgians. It was placed on sale in Belgian shops at highly inflated prices, and largely was ignored by the Belgians because of the high prices or because they could not afford it. The vast majority of all shipments were surreptitiously bought up by the Germans and shipped off to Germany. In other words, money donated by people everywhere for the starving Belgian children mostly ended up assisting the German war effort.

It became a scandal of major proportions and the British and French Governments eventually stepped in and closed down the Commission, using their extensive censorship powers to suppress any news of the scandal being published as it was deemed that this would be bad for morale. It was many years after the war before investigative journalists lifted the lid on this wartime scandal.

At the beginning of 1917 Herbert Hoover, with the Belgian relief scandal blowing up but not yet public knowledge, returned to the United States, now belatedly at war with Germany. He had lived outside America for two decades and was unknown to the public, who were astounded when it was announced that he had been appointed US. Food Administrator - with sweeping powers over the distribution of all food products for the duration of the war. Evidently Hoover had managed to maintain contacts with the powerbrokers of the Republican Party. They appear to have welcomed this multi-millionaire mining expert with open arms without making any serious inquiries about the methods by which he had acquired that wealth. Or perhaps they were aware of it but not concerned as their own methods of wealth-accumulation were not too dissimilar.

After the war, with the Food Administration dissolved he entered political life as Secretary for Commerce under President Harding and then under President Coolidge. When the latter decided to retire, Hoover surprisingly gained the nomination for President and served as a very ineffectual President in the 1929-1933 black depression years. He slipped away from politics after that and lived in seclusion until 1964. When he died that year it surprised most Americans who had forgotten all about him and hadn't realised he was still around.

Ask the average American Republican voter about his presidency and they will respond that he was just plain unlucky to come to office in the period of the Great Depression. The knowledgeable Republicans who have studied their history know better. They know his party dumped on him when, half way through his presidency they found they had bought a political lemon. Because he had been away from America for so long, there was little about him on the record in the USA. He was an unknown and because he maintained such a low profile, little research was done on him.

It was only when he became President in 1929 that the

Democrats started to do serious research, looking for dirt, as is the custom with major political parties everywhere. When they could not find anything in the US they extended their researches overseas, particularly in the UK, and hit pay dirt of the type that Hoover liked to boast about for his mining operations. From 1932 on newspaper and magazine articles and finally books began to hit the streets outlining his numerous financial peccadillos - all to the very considerable embarrassment of the Republican Party. Hoover became the classic lame duck leader no one wanted to know, let alone consider re-electing. He simply vanished into obscurity, after Franklin Roosevelt swept into office with his New Deal. Hoover was stone cold dead politically, if not physically.

So much for the politics. But what about the human side of Hoover? What about that well publicised fling with the barmaid from Hannan's Hotel in Kalgoorlie back in 1898 when he was young and fancy free?

The source of this interesting story is Arthur Reid, who recorded it in his book *Those Were The Days* (Barclay & Sharland, Perth, 1933) when Hoover was still US President. Since Reid provided no evidence for his claim or any provenance for the famous poem that accompanied the story, basing it on personal recollections, it is necessary to take a close look at the source itself.

Reid was a contemporary of Hoover, spending 17 years on the Western Australian goldfields from 1893 to 1910, being there the entire period that Hoover was also active on the goldfields. Reid first came to Coolgardie as a prospector but gave that up after three months to move into journalism. Perhaps he had some prior experience in the Fourth Estate, but he provides few biographical details in his rambling tale of the goldfields.

Initially he was a "stringer" (correspondent) for Perth and Sydney newspapers, reporting daily events on the goldfields. He graduated to reporter on the *Sun*, a lively and widely read Kalgoolie paper, Sunday being the only day the miners had to rest and read up on gossip. He quickly became the paper's editor, then bought a half share in it and finally purchased it outright. He was not only widely known and respected throughout the goldfields during his long stay, he knew everyone of note to visit or work on the fields in that time because of his profession.

Herbert Hoover was well known to him, but no more so than a a score or more prominent personalities who shaped the destiny the goldfields. He was not a critic of Hoover, and when writing his memories late in life seems to have been a bit in awe of the fact that he had once known a man who later became President of the United States of America. So far as I know, Reid is the only person to have written, if ever so briefly, of Hoover the person , as distinct from his mine work, while he was on the goldfields.

Reid described Hoover as a very reserved person, but an indefatigable worker, and a person who had to be a leader or nothing. In this respect he compared him with (President) Theodore ("Teddy") Roosevelt. Reid quotes a letter which the President's son Kismet wrote to his mother after accompanying his father on an African game hunt: "You know Mother", he wrote, "Father will never go to a wedding because he can't be the bride; neither will he attend a funeral because he can't be the corpse."

Reid's comments on Hoover as a person were made in a chapter on Hannan's Hotel at Kalgoorlie. This was the favourite watering hole and social centre of the entire goldf ields. Reid noted that Hoover was a frequent visitor to Hannan's Hotel while he was manager of the Sons of Gwa1ior mine at Leonora. Confirmation of this is given in Martyn and Audrey Webb's massive history of Kalgoorlie) *Golden Destiny*. The Webbs record that while Hoover was managing Sons of Gwalior, he lived at No 6 Elizabeth Street, the 'Nob Hill' area of Kalgoorlie.

Reid concluded his chapter by saying that years after leaving the goldf ields, Hoover addressed the following erotic and exotic verses to a former Hannan's barmaid:

Do you ever dream my sweetheart, of a twilight long ago,
Of a park in old Kalgoorlie, where the bougainvilleas grow,
Where the moonbeams on the pathways trace a shimmering brocade
And the overhanging peppers form a lovers' promenade.
Where in soft cascades of cadence from a garden close at hand,
Came the murmurous mellow music of a sweet orchestral band,
Years have flown since then, my sweetheart, fleet as orchard blooms in May;
But the hour that fills my dreaming, was it only yesterday?
Stood we two a space in silence, while the summer sun slipped down,
And the grey dove dusk with drooping pinions wrapt the mining town.
Then you raised your tender glances darkly, dreamily to mine,
And my pulses clashed like symbols in a rhapsody divine.
And the pent-up fires of longing loosed their prison's weak control,
And in wild hot words came rushing madly from my burning soul.
Wild hot words that spoke of passion, hitherto but half expressed,
And I clasped you close my sweetheart, kissed you, strained you to my breast,
While the starlight spangled heavens rolled around us where we stood,
And a tide of bliss swept surging through the currents of our blood,
And I spent my soul in kisses, crushed upon your scarlet mouth.
Oh! my red-lipped sunbrowned sweetheart, dark-eyed daughter of the south.
It was well that fate should part us, it was well my path should lead,
Back to slopes of high endeavour aye, and was it well indeed.
You have wed some southern squatter, learned long since his every whim
Soothed his sorrows, borne his troubles. sung your sweetest songs for him.
I have fought my fight and triumphed, on the map I've writ my name,

But I prize one hour of loving, more than fifty years of fame.
It was but a summer madness, that possessed me, men will hold,
And the yellow moon bewitched me, with its wizardry of gold,
As they will, but oft times in the dusk, I close my eyes
And in dreams drift back where stars rain silver splendour from the skies,
To a park in far Kalgoorlie, where the golden wattles grow,
Where you kissed me in the twilight, of a summer long ago.
And I clasp you close, my sweetheart, while each throbbing pulse is thrilled
By a low and mournful music that shall never more be stilled.

Wow! What a girl! They don't make barmaids like that any more – not even in Kalgoorlie.

But, and this is a very big but; did Herbert Hoover pen that piece of verse as Reid claimed? It seems highly unlikely, given his taciturn nature and distinct lack of any claims to literary standards. And when was it supposed to have been written and how did it fall into Reid's hands? Reid provides no answer other than to make the comment that it was written "years after Hoover left the goldfields". Reid's book was published in 1933, placing it before that date, not later in Hoover's retirement years. Would a man of Hoover's natural caution and political ambitions have penned such a piece while on the long journey up to the White House? Anyway, would ANY man have been silly enough to write such a poem while his wife was still alive?

If your answer to the above questions is a resounding "NO" -as my inclination is, then you have to cast around elsewhere for the likely author. And I suggest that you may not have to look beyond Arthur Reid himself. Reid was a wordsmith by profession and the flow of this poem indicates an author who was very good at descriptive phrases and imagery. In fact it is a very good poem of its genre. And Reid certainly fancied himself as a bit of a bush balladist judging by the large number of poems (his and others) which he scattered through the pages of his book.

My guess is that Reid knew of Hoover's affair with the barmaid, but didn't want to give graphic details in journalistic form. After all he was writing in the 1930's, when Hoover was still US President. I think he hit on the idea of putting it across in a poem which carried a huge amount of innuendo but really said so little in a factual sense that he would have been perfectly safe from any libel action.

Perhaps Hoover himself was not romantically carried away to the extent that our anonymous poet imagined. In 1898 when he received news from Moreing that he was to go to China on a $15,000 a year assignment, the dark-eyed barmaid was consigned to the back seat of his life. He immediately cabled Lou Henry back in Monterey, USA, asking her to marry him. Reid records that a cable came back immediately with the brief answer "Whenever you are ready". And that was that as far as the barmaid was concerned.

Hoover immediately took a ship to London for briefings on his mission to China. He then crossed the Atlantic for a reunion with Lou Henry, whom he had met while at Stanford University. Lou Henry was doing the same geology course as Hoover, but two years behind him. She had completed the course successfully and held the same Diploma - though hers was earned on merit; Hoover's had been obtained by deception. It is probably the only time that an American President and the First Lady have had identical tertiary qualifications.

Arthur Reid records that at the time Hoover was living in Kalgoolie (and wooing the barmaid) he was a Quaker. Apparently he abandoned these beliefs on his way back to the States because when he and Lou Henry married on February 10 1899, at Monterey, it was in a Roman Catholic Church. The couple sailed for Shanghai the following day and spent their honeymoon at sea. No offspring resulted from the union.

All of which raises an interesting question. Let your imagination take flight for a moment into the realm of "the land of what might have been". Just suppose that the summer madness at Kalgoorlie on those steamy starlit nights had been just a bit stronger, to the extent that young Hoover had ditched Lou Henry in favour of Hannan's barmaid. Wouldn't that have been a turn up for the books further down the line? A Kalgoorlie ex-barmaid as America's First Lady in the White House? What would the Society ladies of Washington thought about that? And what sort of a feeding frenzy would the paparazzi of the period have gone into had they done a bit of delving and come across **that** poem while Hoover was still in the White House?

And I can't help wondering whether the dark-eyed Kalgoorlie beauty really married her squatter? And did she have any dark-eyed offspring? Are any of them still around anywhere? If so what do they now think of their Mum's fling with Herbert Hoover, one time President of the United States?

10

The Mystery Axeman

It is a very frustrating experience to pose a question to which there is no certain answer since the facts have been lost in the mists of time.

This very much applies to a tree stump housed in the small folk museum at Wentworth in the far west of New South Wales. Who chopped the bloody thing down? But you will ask in vain because there is no certain answer, only guesses - and some of them pretty wild and improbable - for this tree poses a genuine mystery about the early exploration of southern Australia.

There are actually two trees involved in this intriguing exhibit at the Wentworth Museum, one within the other. The larger trunk is a huge Redgum with a girth just on fifteen feet from a tree on the junction of the Darling and Murray Rivers sawn off by the NSW Forestry Commission on February 3 1971. From the growth rings the Forestry Commission experts assess the tree as having been at least two hundred years old at the time it was felled.

This giant Redgum did not stand alone. It grew around the stump of a much earlier and older tree. This smaller tree originally sprouted two stumps almost from ground level, each with a diameter of approximately ten inches. And the puzzling feature of these two smaller stumps is that they were felled by an axe. There is no doubt on this score as the axe cuts are quite clear, even after this great span of time.

Since the Redgum is adjudged by the experts to be at least two hundred years old when felled, this puts the age of the smaller two-pronged tree in its core well beyond the period of white settlement in 1788. In fact the first white man to visit the area was Charles Sturt in 1830 and his party certainly did not chop the old tree down as the Redgum's growth would have been well advanced by the time of his exploration of the area. Nor could the old tree have been fell by aborigines who did not possess axes.

Who then, did chop it down?

One theory advanced by locals is that it may have been Maoris who are thought to have visited the area before the period of white settlement as New Zealand greenstones were found in the area by early settlers. Whilst Maoris may have made unrecorded visits to our shores in the 18th Century they did not possess axes of the kind needed to fell our hardwoods.

Abel Tasman certainly sailed across the southern part of Australia in 1642 but his voyage is well charted and he sailed far to the south of the Victorian coastline before discovering and naming Tasmania. It is extremely unlikely that his crew cut down the old mystery Wentworth tree.

But there were other visitors to Victoria's southern coastline more than a hundred years before Abel Tasman passed that way - three Portuguese caravels led by Critovao de Mendonca. And to explain how they came to be in this area in a highly secret voyage, we must go back even further into history.

When Christopher Columbus discovered the Americas in 1492

he sparked off the biggest land grab in history amongst all the European powers. This eventually led to bitter rivalry between two important Catholic nations, the mighty Spain and its much smaller neighbour Portugal. The disputes over rival territorial claims towards the end of the 15th Century were so intense that war between these two Catholic nations seemed imminent. This alarmed Pope Alexander Vl who brokered a deal between the two nations which was aimed at keeping each in his own backyard, as it were. Under the Treaty of Tordesillas signed in 1494 a line was drawn down a map of what was then the known world which was to be a demarcation line which kept each power from exploring or occupying the other's territory. In the Pacific what became known as the Pope's line gave Portugal Timor and Macau (which it had by then claimed) plus the western third of what is now Australia, but then completely uncharted territory.

Both sides openly and covertly breached the Treaty in succeeding decades but warfare did not break out as both sides gave at least token acknowledgment to the Pope's wishes.

However, all goodwill by Portugal came to an end in 1518 when King Manoelli received information that a Spanish flotilla led by Magellan was about to sail into the Pacific from the East to establish Empire outposts in the East Indies where Portugal had enjoyed a monopoly. Portugal sent two squadrons of warships out in search of Magellan's fleet but was unable to locate it, so they strengthened their outposts of Goa, Macau and Timor.

To try and forestall any Spanish claims to the "great south land" (ie. Australia) the Portuguese also dispatched from Timor a fleet of three caravels under the command of Captain Cristovao de Mendonca, with Captain Pedro Eanes, second-in-command. Their mission was to chart the Great South Land, especially the east coast, all in flagrant breach of the Treaty of Tortdesillas since this was all on the Spanish side of the demarcation line of the Pope's map. Mendonca also had instructions to search for legendary "Islands of Gold" supposed to be tucked away in or near the Great South Land.

Mendonca's small fleet sailed off some time in 1521 and quite by accident bypassed the huge island of New Guinea (which at that time was unknown to both the Portuguese and Spanish) and managed to sail through the Torres Strait without knowing he had done so! He was now at the tip of Terra Australis Incognita, so he proceeded down the east coast in the reverse direction to that taken by Captain Cook, the so-called discoverer of the east coast, more than two and a half centuries later.

Mendonca carefully charted his way down the east coast, then turning west when he reached the bottom of the continent. He probably would have circumnavigated the continent, a remarkable feat for that age, but disaster struck somewhere along the Victorian coastline, probably in the vicinity of where Warnambool now stands, as he lost one of his caravels in unexplained circumstances. At that point his charts abruptly cease and it is assumed that he backtracked all the way back up the east coast to Timor. His charts and reports of this remarkable voyage eventually found their way into the secret naval archives in Lisbon where they remained out of sight of inquisitive rivals for more than four centuries. It is only in recent decades that some, and only some, of these documents have emerged for study by historians.

During the last century, there were various sightings of the remains of what is now assumed to be Mendonca's lost caravel - the so-called Mahogany ship, amongst the sand dunes of the Victorian coastline. But settlers in the last century had other things than old wrecks on their minds and time and the elements covered up the old ship, which is still being sought by modern explorers.

How long Mendonca tarried along the Victorian coast after he lost his third caravel is not known. But it is quite possible that he would have done some further exploring, if not charting, of the coastline. The mouth of the Murray is not all that far from old sightings of the Mahogany Ship and it is by no means inconceivable that he might have sent a party up the Murray to its junction with the Darling, where the old mystery Redgum once stood. And if he needed a couple of replacement masts, his crew might well have been the axemen who chopped down those two old branches whose remains now sit on the floor of the Wentworth Museum - stumps which aeons later were enveloped in a womb-like condition of the giant Redgum cut down in 1971.

This is all speculation, of course, but when you do not have any positive answers to a puzzle is there a better guess to the question: Who DID cut that tree down?

11

The Vegemite Kids

Modern nutritionists are forever telling us that "we are what we eat", but their message is not new. Away back in the 19th Century novelist Marcus Clarke observed that " ...the quality of a race is determined by two things: food and climate".

If Clarke and the nutritionists are right, then it explains much about some of the inhabitants, past and present, of the Sunburnt Country as our diet since White Settlement has at times been distinctly odd if not downright dangerous.

The early settlers suffered much from Barcoo Rot and other unpleasant ailments as a result of eating nardoo seed, on which the natives seemed to thrive. They had more success in digesting the traditional bush damper, but no one has yet come forward with claims that a diet of damper and black billy tea can sustain the inner man for any length of time.

Quite early in the piece the bush cooks turned their attention to pies, but their early efforts were not exactly gourmet achievements. Brunton Stephens in *My Other Chinese Cook* wrote of one Chinese chef:

He was lazy, he was cheeky
He was dirty, he was sly,
But he had a single virtue,
And its name was rabbit pie.

However, as the tale progressed it turned out that the contents of these pies were not rabbits but were provided by a litter of pups on the station. Other known contents of early bush pies have included possums, bandicoots, catfish, crocodiles and indeed anything that walked, crawled, jumped or otherwise moved. Since those far off days the pie-makers have moved into top gear to serve the insatiable appetite for pies expressed by a nation that likes to eat on the run. Millions of the bloody things are produced and sold every day of the week to be consumed with or without lashings of tomato sauce and other condiments. They come in various shapes, circular and square, and in some odd forms such as the South Australian specialty of a pie floating in a swamp of pea soup, known as a Floater.

While meat pies have been around for centuries in other parts of the world, only Australia has converted them into a national take-away dish. But then we have been quite inventive with other foods of dubious nutritional value.

The damper has been mentioned but other early distinctive foods have included the Johnny Cake, Bully Beef, and the Lamington. For a long time we laid claim to the invention of the Pavlova, but New Zealand blew us out of the water on that one producing hard evidence that it had its birthplace across the Tasman. A more modern invention the Chico roll had its birthplace on our shores, as did Golden Syrup ("Cocky's Joy") , along with the habit of burning all nutritional value out of meat by throwing it on the barbie.

But there is one nutritional invention that stands out head and shoulders above all the aforementioned foods as a gastronomic icon of Australia - if for no other reason that no other country appears to want a bar of it - and that is VEGEMITE.

Vegemite is a pure concentrated yeast extract which is produced in the form of a thick paste. When introduced to it most visitors to these shores take one sniff, curl their lips and back off rapidly. Seldom can they be persuaded to even give it a try. But it has a special place in the hearts (and stomachs) of the locals and one can only conclude that exposure to it from childhood has given the population a form of addiction, even to the extent they have been known to automatically pack a jar or two of the stuff in their suitcases when travelling abroad, and to send parcels of it to friends and relatives stranded in some Vegemite-less part of the globe. In 1977 when singer Helen Reddy returned to Australia after a long sojourn abroad she explained the reason for her journey home in simple terms: "I ran out of Vegemite."

During World War II the Australian Army had seven pound tins of the stuff made up and shipped to our frontline troops serving up in the islands. Which raises quite a few questions. Did the troops actually EAT the stuff in this quantity? Or did they open up the tins and try to smoke or smell the Japs out of their fox-holes with it? Or did they use the tins as lethal weapons to throw at the advancing enemy when they had expended their ammunition? Unfortunately the Army records are silent on these points.

And it seems that back in the war years Vegemite even got unfairly mixed up in the rather unsavoury cross fire of sectarian prejudices which beset Australia in those days. We have evidence for this in Barry Oakley's book *Scribbling in the Dark*, reminiscences of his childhood and early life. In 1943 Oakley was a pupil at the Christian Brothers College, St Kilda, Melbourne, and has vivid memories of a lay teacher named Mr Ward, who apparently was a sectarian warrior of the old school, not prepared to yield an inch where the enemy (ie. all non-Catholics) was concerned. As related by Oakley, Mr Ward would fossick out a Vegemite sandwich being consumed by one his charges, point his pipe at the offending object, and trumpet loudly for all to hear:

"This boy has Vegemite in his sandwiches. This boy is helping the enemy. You didn't know that, did you boy?. If you want to help the Seventh Day Adventists go on. Eat your Kornies. Tuck into your Vegemite. You just go right ahead".

In these outbursts Mr Ward was not only being a bigot, he was dead wrong on the factual side, because Vegemite was then, and still is, produced by Kraft. His enemies, the Seventh Day Adventists, were the producers of Vegemite's deadly rival in the market place, Marmite. The Seventh Day Adventists would have been upset no end by Mr Ward's outbursts, not so much by his bigotry, but his enormous error of aligning them with a rival product they loathed and daily waged war against in the shops of the nation. And the reason for their antipathy to Vegemite was based on a feeling that they had somehow been cheated in the race for the hearts, minds and stomachs of the Australian populace on the spread front. Marmite had been on the market several years before Kraft came up with Vegemite (in 1923) and promptly stolen their customers with more aggressive advertising.

Initially Marmite had been so successful that a rival (not Kraft) had brought out a similar product named PAWILL and had promoted it under the slogan of "Marmite, but Pawill", only to sink without trace, and deservedly, under the weight of this dreadful pun.

Which doesn't throw much light on our dietary habits, though it may explain why some unkind folk on the other side of the world tend to regard us as a nation of rather uncouth vegemites!

12

A Piece of Desiccated Tissue

The most important world event of 1815 undoubtedly was the Battle of Waterloo which resulted in the surrender to the British of Napoleon Bonaparte

Once they had him, what to do with him? Where to imprison him?

These questions must have exercised the tiny brains of the British establishment no end in the months that followed. It must have dawned on them that Australia was the obvious place for the exile of their distinguished prisoner. The unpleasantness of the Rum Rebellion, and overthrow of Governor Bligh, was long in the past and the colony was stable and thriving under Macquarie. And the French could hardly mount a rescue mission to the Antipodes.

Inexplicably they settled not on Terra Australis but on the much nearer and more vulnerable island of St Helena. Australia thus missed out on acquiring a quite unique souvenir which might well have enabled us to solve all our Balance of Payment Problems!

When Napoleon died in 1821 there was a rumour that he may have been poisoned so , to be on the safe side, the Brits had the exEmperor's doctor Antommarchi perform an autopsy. This was carried out in the presence of the Abbe Vignale, who had earlier administered the last rites to Napoleon.

During the autopsy the doctor removed what he delicately described as a "small tendon" (apparently Napoleon was not well-endowed, which perhaps explains his well-known "Not tonight, Josephine" utterance). Abbe Vignale carried away from the operation table this rather unique souvenir and added it to a not inconsiderable collection of other memorabilia which Napoleon had given him, or he had otherwise acquired. All these items he subsequently took back to France.

Connoisseurs of such matters were aware of the unusual nature of the Abbe's collection but the matter did not become public until 1924 when the noted London booksellers Maggs Brothers sold the collection intact to the flamboyant American book and art dealer Doctor Abraham Simon Wolf Rosenbach for the relatively modest sum of four hundred pounds sterling.

Dr Rosenbach was interested in only one item in the collection, the tendon which by that time had become a "piece of desiccated tissue". The colourful doctor announced his find to the press as "a muscle tendon from the groin", the nearest euphemism he could get away with in that prudish era. He proceeded to milk a million dollars worth of publicity from his purchase when he displayed his Napoleonic collection in New York Museum of French Art.

A contemporary newspaper report of the event noted: "...women giggled as they saw in a glass case something looking like a maltreated strip of buckskin shoelace or shrivelled eel".

Poor Napoleon. Never in history has such intimate portion's of such a noted man's anatomy been shown to so many.

Dr Rosenbach dined out for many a year on the story of his unusual gallic souvenir, but eventually he tired of the object and sold it to a wealthy American collector. In recent years it has been in the possession of a well known American urologist, who no doubt uses it as one of the "tools of his trade".

But the mind keeps wandering back to the realm of "what might have been" if Napoleon had been sent to a different exile and he been able to point his Percy at Botany Bay Porcelain. The chances of that particular Percy staying on here would have been so much stronger.

Imagine what those imaginative chaps and chapesses down at the Powerhouse Museum could acieve if they had been able to get their ever-itching fingers on such a relic

Set up under glass in a dimly lit room (extra entry charge twenty dollars) and the Japanese tourists and the money would roll in. Certainly enough to balance our national debt after a year or two of good tourist seasons.

13

A Military Manoeuvre

MANOEUVRE: A planned and regulated movement or evolution of troops ...an adroit move; skilful proceeding to manipulate with skill or adroitness... to scheme, intrigue etc.

A question for Military Buffs: Name the Australian soldier responsible for conceiving, planning, organising and executing the most successful military manoeuvre of World War 11 as understood by the above quoted dictionary definition.

After much scratching of heads no doubt a large number of names will be proffered in response to this question. But I very much doubt that any such list will contain my nomination for this honour: Corporal Gary Coutts.

Corporal WHO? you may well ask.

And if you sought an answer from Army histories you would seek in vain. He was the cause of so many red faces amongst the Army Brass of World War 11 that they simply want to forget him and his outrageous Military Manoeuvre in the summer of 1942-3.

Corporal Coutts was a member of the North Australia Observer Unit (NAOU), known far and wide by the extremely derogatory label of Curtin's Cowboys. During the war the Army managed to conceal from the public, by tight censorship controls, the very existence of the unit. And after the war a wall of silence descended on what the Brass conceived to be an ill-conceived, ghastly military mistake.

The curtains would have remained drawn had not Richard and Helen Walker written a very well-researched and presented account of the whole operation under the title *Curtin's Cowboys - Australia's Secret Bush Commandos* (Allen & Unwin 1986).

NAOU was the brainchild of Professor WEH Stanner, an anthropologist who early in 1942 was personal assistant to the Minister for the Army, Frank Forde. The Japanese were bombing the living daylights out of Darwin and were expected to invade Australia from the north at any time. As Stanner had made many field trips through the northern parts of Australia in the pre-war years, and had close contacts with aboriginal groups, he was asked to prepare a report on what might be done on a military level should the Japanese invade.

Professor Stanner suggested that small commando groups with radios should be used to infiltrate behind the lines of invading forces to observe and report on enemy positions, even though it was inevitable that most of these units would be detected and executed. They were to be expendable. The first Australian Kamikaze units!.

Hasty conferences followed and to Professor Stanner's astonishment the idea was not only adopted, but he was told he was to organise it pronto and command it with the rank of Major (he had no military background or training at all).

Thus was born NAOU. A force of five hundred men, all volunteers, was quickly cobbled together. The requirements set down for the force included medical fitness, bush experience, horsemanship (since this was largely a mounted unit), skills with guns and (preferably) signals training. They were to be formed into small radio patrol units, and sent to outposts (with aboriginal guides) right across a territory spanning more than 3000 kilometres from the Gulf country to Broome.

All this was achieved in record time (for an army) and soon the NAOU force was scattered over a vast area of the continent. Because of the time frame, and the disbursement into small self-contained units, there was no overall training and the Nackeroos, as they were nicknamed, quickly gained the reputation of being the most undisciplined unit of the Australian Army. Initially morale was high because the recruits believed they were going into action. But the Japanese refused to cooperate by invading the country.

The Nackeroos soon woke up to the fact that action had passed them by; that they were doing it tough in some of the worst conditions imaginable without hope of sighting an enemy soldier. With the approach of the end of year wet season morale quickly plummeted, especially when all applications to join fighting units were rejected. The Army should have quickly disbanded NAOU once the danger of invasion had passed, but simply put it all in the too hard basket.

It was then that Corporal Coutts, inactive in a remote camp at Roper Bar, came up with an idea. Why don't some of us take the Blitz Waggon, head down south to the city, and give ourselves up as a group and demand we be recruited into fighting units?

Corporal Coutts, who was then 27, a seasoned traveller, and described as a "tough cookie,' found many willing recruits for his wild idea, so he set about detailed, meticulous planning for the breakout.

The big problem was petrol as the camp vehicle, the big three-ton Chevrolet blitz buggy, was a fuel guzzler requiring constant topping up. This problem was solved when a truck driven by a Danish migrant came through with supplies, and the Dane was persuaded to part with his petrol requisition book!

Corporal Coutts' party comprised another corporal and ten privates. They managed to park the blitz buggy out of sight of the camp and loaded it secretly with food and some 44 gallon drums of fuel. They set off immediately after roll call on the evening of November 30 1942 with everyone in the camp except the senior officer creating diversions, knowing they had twelve hours start before being discovered. In that period they covered a very respectable 250 kilometres, reaching Matarinka by daybreak.

With the dawn their flight was discovered and the radio operator was instructed to send out the alarm. Being in on the plan, he gave them the valuable time they needed by sending the message out on the wrong frequency, and giving a description of a different type of truck (a Ford Blitz truck). By evening he became worried and transmitted the message on the right frequency, thus triggering alarms throughout the army network, with roadblocks established and patrols out seeking the miscreants heading south.

But Corporal Coutts wasn't heading for Adelaide as he had told everyone He was putting his master plan into action by heading east over rough bush tracks with his target Brisbane 3400 kilometres away, all without any maps, compass or any member of his small crew having been over the route. They were flying blind by the seat of their pants through some of the world's roughest country with early rains from the wet season already turning the bush tracks into quagmires.

And by a combination of incredible luck, crazy bluffs and sheer guts they made it in the truck to a point near Mitchell in Queensland where on a back road their sump was torn out by a tree trunk which had fallen across the road. They trudged back into Mitchell, told a story of a breakdown, were feted and fed by the locals and next day put on a troop train heading for Brisbane (with a hamper of food provided by the locals for their journey!).

They reached Brisbane exactly 16 days after starting their incredible journey, only to run into a dead end when every Provost they encountered disbelieved their story and told them to "get lost". Finally they caught a tram to Kelvin Grove, where the Provost Barracks were located, only to encounter a similar reception from the sergeant in charge. Only when they insisted, did he look up the records and find the report of them going AWL 16 days earlier.

At this stage the officer in charge of the Provosts, Lieutenant Colonel Joe ("Jerusalem Joe") Courtney, was brought into the picture to listen to their story. He kept them in open arrest at the barracks while he tried to implement a scheme he had worked out, involving them all initially enlisting (temporarily) in the Provosts and then being quietly transferred over to fighting units.

The Army Brass would not have a bar of this and insisted that Courtney send them all back to their unit under heavy guard to face the music, "Bugger that," said Jerusalem Joe, a very forthright bloke, and after allowing them out of the barracks for a few quiet beers, he shook their hands, wished them good luck, and provided them with passes to get them back to the Northern Territory under their own steam.

The Dirty Dozen, as no doubt the Army was by then calling them, retraced their steps by train and army trucks over the 3400 kilometres, reaching the NAOU Headquarters at Katherine on January 6 1943, causing an immense stir when it was discovered that they had travelled all the way on their own and were all present.

And did that soften the boot-leather thick hearts of the Army Brass?

Not on your Nelly. The Army threw the book at them. They

were court martialled with the two corporals copping 180 days and the ten privates each 150 days, to be served in the Brocks Creek Detention Centre where the policy was to break the spirit of the men and crush the slightest signs of rebellion. This was mainly achieved by a physical round of fifteen pack drills with full 60lbs of gear each day (in the tropical heat of the monsoon season) and on a diet comprising army biscuits which had been soaked in boiling water until they became a sort of porridge. They were given a large ladle of this goo three times a day. On Sundays, as a treat, there was a smear of jam across the top of the porridge.

In the end they only served half their sentences as after 90 days for the corporals and 75 days for the privates, they were taken out and given the option of transferring to other units. Two of the privates stayed with the NAOU and the rest shipped out to fighting units, ceasing to be counted as Nackeroos.

In July 1943 the NAOU was dramatically reduced in size and operation, and by the end of the year it was disbanded with the few remaining Curtin's Cowboys being dispersed among other Army units.

And the Army Brass in unison were heard to mutter: "Amen".

14

Chidley's Answer

Many an individual has got into deep trouble by asking the wrong (or inconvenient) question. But it is also possible to land up the creek without a paddle by providing the wrong (or troublesome) answer to a question.

No one would have known this better than Chidley the Reformer because his answers consistently landed him in deep, deep trouble with the law and the society of his day, a society that tolerated his food and dress reforms, but took violent exception to his sex reforms, despite the fact that these would have resulted in less (not more) sexual activity in the world.

Chidley was born in Melbourne (parentage unknown) and was adopted out of a foundling home by one John James Chidley, who named his adopted son William James, after the American philosopher Chidley senior was an interesting and eccentric character who migrated to Australia from England in the 1850's, settling in Melbourne where (to use his own words) he "got into bad habits" - presumably of a sexual nature.

He decided that marriage might be the way to extricate himself from the situation so he looked around for a partner. He recalled that on the boat out from England there were two spinster sisters with whom he had been friendly so he sought them out, proposed to one and was accepted.

In later life he told his adopted son William that he had never been in love with his wife but that the marriage had worked out reasonably well and had cured him of his "bad habits". However, when his wife died he drifted back to these "bad habits" so he married his wife's sister to effect a new cure.

After a spell on the goldfields unsuccessfully seeking his fortune, he returned to Melbourne with his bride (the first one) and opened a toy shop, which prospered. Soon he had a chain of these shops and as they brought him into contact with state orphanages he ended up adopting five orphans, including the above-mentioned William James.

Chidley senior returned to England with his wife and young family, but several ventures there were unsuccessful and when William James was five the family returned to Melbourne and Chidley senior became an itinerant photographer roaming the Western districts for several years. Chidley senior was a strict vegetarian and seems to have passed on to his adopted off-spring some way out ideas on the subject of sex - particularly in that Victoria era. At one time the family lived in a "share-all" Melbourne Bohemian Commune until internal squabbling and objections by Mrs Chidley put an end to the experiment.

Young William James had a spasmodic education and after leaving school was apprenticed to an architect. He did not complete the four year apprenticeship but the training he received as a draughtsman stood him in good stead as he found he had sufficient artistic flair to earn a reasonable living touring Victoria and South Australian rural districts doing water color and crayon portraits.

Later he turned his talents to professional photography, becoming expert in the fields of developing, enlarging and retouching when the art of photography was in its infancy.

Had he kept to this profession all would have been well, but throughout his teens and twenties he had twin problems of coping with the demon grog and what he described as excessive and enormous sexual appetites. He suffered considerable pangs of guilt over excessive self-abuse, that good old Victorian euphemism for masturbation.

Much of his experience seems to have been with prostitutes which resulted in him contracting gonorrhoea. When he was 23 he became addicted in a new form when he "got religion" and was baptised by Bishop Short in Adelaide Cathedral.

This conversion prompted him to adopt a completely new lifestyle when he joined a travelling playgroup called The Byron Comedy Company which toured South Australian districts bringing culture to the locals. With the group was an actress Ada Grantleigh with whom he forged an on and off relationship which lasted more than two decades, though they never married. Ada had two unsuccessful marriages behind her so the question of bigamy probably loomed large in her calculations. However, in the periods they were together they invariably travelled as Mr and Mrs Chidley.

According to Chidley (in his autobiographical *Confessions*) Ada had an insatiable appetite for sex, drink and meat, three failings which caused eternal rows in their turbulent relationship.

During one of their partings, Ada gave birth in Adelaide to a male child who died soon afterwards. By coincidence the woman in the adjoining bed to Ada at the hospital had died during the childbirth but her male baby had survived, so Ada took him home, "adopted" him and bestowed on him the name of Donald Chidley (such incidents were commonplace in the last century).

When Ada was reconciled with Chidley she told him that Donald was his offspring and it was some years before she confessed the truth to him. Donald was never told the truth and went to his grave believing he was Chidley's son.

In 1899 Chidley accepted a job in New Zealand and soon saved enough money to send for Ada and Donald (known to the couple as "Pad"). The venture was a disaster and "Pad" proved such a handful in his new country, constantly running away from home and committing petty crimes that the couple abandoned him to a juvenile institution at Burnham, near Christchurch, and returned to Australia. They never saw "Pad" again though they kept in touch by correspondence.

When Ada died in Melbourne on December 1 1908, aged 48, from the ravages of heavy drinking and epileptic seizures, Chidley was devastated. He immediately gave up both drinking and sex and threw himself into a furious bout of writing, first completing his *Confessions* (which Havelock Ellis described as "...far the most remarkable thing - indeed the only thing - that has come out of Australia"), and a much more modest work entitled *The Answer* which outlined his various theories on Dress, Food and Sex, publication of which was to land him in headlong confrontation with society of the day.

His theories on Food were innocuous enough since they were merely a variation on the widely promoted vegetarian beliefs of the era (Chidley advocated a strict diet of fruit and nuts). His views on dress were a shade more controversial especially when he took to walking the streets in the garment he advocated as the most practical for Australia's climate - a type of Roman toga extending to the kneeline. This brought derisory comments from passers by, but no real problems. It merely branded him as an eccentric in the eyes of the public.

New and even strange theories on food and dress, the public could wear, even tolerate. New theories on sex however, was a different matter - and it was here that Chidley came unstuck in a big way.

To understand why this was so it is necessary to know something of Chidley's own problems in this area. These days when a major political figure such as US President Bill Clinton is exposed as a compulsive womaniser he is said to have "Trouser Trouble". And some very prominent 20th Century males have been so classified, figures such as John F Kennedy, Lloyd George, Mao Tse Tung and a couple of Australian post-war Prime Ministers to name just a few.

Chidley also had "Trouser Trouble" but his infliction was different to that of the figures mentioned above. Chidley's problem was a medical affliction known as Priapism (from the Greek Priapus, God of Male Fertility), bouts of prolonged and quite painful erection of the penis caused by neurological disorders or obstruction of the penile blood vessels. The extraordinary thing about Chidley's condition was that he experienced his first attack of Priapism at the tender age of five when he was living with this adoptive parents in England. When they became aware of the problem, they called in a doctor, but that worthy had never encountered the condition before and could offer no remedies apart from a "wait and see" policy. Such childhood attacks of Priapism are known to medical science, though quite rare, so the young Chidley was left to deal on his own with what is nowadays a treatable complaint. In his *Confessions* he recalled how he had reacted to the initial attack:

I stood in the corner by the fireplace, face to the wall, refusing to let him (the doctor) touch 'It '. I remember my rage and shame, and Mother's kind words - even the amused look in the young doctor's eyes as he dabbed at 'It' with a sponge, which increased my rage so that I kicked at him.

Back in Australia, Chidley was sent off to school where further attacks of Priapism were the cause of much anguish. On one occasion he brought a toilet seat down on the offending member, only to cause great pain and subsequent bruising. while on another occasion he tried to cut his penis off with a knife. But this attempt at self-Bobbitting himself also failed and only resulted in him having a permanently scarred member.

In his *Confessions* Chidley is silent on the subject of whether his priapic condition continued into adulthood. However, given the trauma it produced so early in his life, it is perhaps not surprising that he should have come to the conclusion that all the ills of Homo Sapiens were due to the male erection. If Chidley had left the matter there and merely advocated celibacy as a solution to mankind's ills, all might have been plain sailing. He would, of course, have been advocating the long term extinction of Homo Sapiens, but at least he would have been on a similar wave length to the followers of Malthus and the Chinese Communists in their persistent but fruitless efforts at population control.

But on one occasion Chidley had achieved a satisfactory sexual union with Ada without (or so he claimed) an erection being involved. It happened once, and only once, during a reunion after one of their many partings. Both were lying naked on a hotel bed discussing their problems, sex not being on their minds at the time, when the couple found to their mutual surprise that Chidley's flaccid penis had somehow found its way into Ada's vagina. Apparently intercourse of a new and stimulating variety followed. They were never able to duplicate the experience, but it left a deep impression on Chidley and led him to undertake a study of the animal world. Following visits to the Zoo, he claimed to have found that monkeys (among other animals) had sex without the males having a full erection.

Based on such slight "evidence" as his one-time experience with Ada and his Zoological observations, he came up with a rather weird theory that Mankind should avoid their present day methods of coition (which he claimed were harmful to both men and women) and develop a new form of sex involving vaginal suction rather than a male erection. He put it this way: "Thus the female vagina and womb must have the power of becoming erect and distended with its sphincter closed forming a vacuum, and yet, like the duck's, it must flash open when the penis touches the clitoris, drawing the penis in by a rush of air." This unusual act he described as "the winking of the vulva", and thought that it could only take place in the Spring, the coupling season, and then only between lovers!

Having reached this conclusion, Chidley wrote: "I had made the discovery that will some day save the world from all its misery".

Such was Chidley's crusading nature that he could not keep such a discovery to himself. He had to go out and proclaim it from the rooftops - in this case by writing a small 48 page booklet, *The Answer*, which set out his theories on Food and Dress (briefly) and on Sex in some detail.

The first edition of *The Answer* appeared in Melbourne in 1911, and was mainly sold by Chidley for one and sixpence at his Yarra Bank rallies. Spouting radical sex theories from a public soap box was one thing. Setting them out in print was another, and the Melbourne gendarmes quickly moved in and arrested Chidley and seized all copies of *The Answer* they could lay their hands on. Booksellers who had had the temerity to stock it were given plain warnings that they would be prosecuted if they displayed it. It quickly disappeared under the counters.

Finding Melbourne distinctly unfriendly to his message, Chidley hastily moved himself and his small remaining stock of books to Sydney, believing that city to be more liberal-minded than the bleak city of the south. He was sadly mistaken, as the Wallopers of the north were to prove no more friendly than their southern counterparts, possibly due to the fact that at that period the New South Wales police force, like that of "New York's Finest" was heavily stacked with Irish Catholics who regarded ANY discussion of sexual matters to fall into the category of public acts of indecency. The fact that Chidley's weird theory would, if adopted, result in considerably LESS sexual activity, not more bonking, was irrelevant. It was just that in that age sex was not something to be discussed from the soap box or in print.

The persecution of Chidley occurred almost as soon as he set foot in Sydney - and persecution is not too harsh a word to describe what followed - mainly as a result of the then Chief Secretary and Minister for Public Health, Mr George ("Baldy") Black, MLA, taking a personal interest in the matter and directing the police offensive against the reformer. He did so on moral grounds, a notable piece of hypocrisy given Black's own reputation and character.

Black had arrived in Sydney from Scotland in 1873 at the age of 19. On the voyage out he had seduced a Mrs Duggan, wife of a fellow passenger, and on reaching Sydney set up house with her. In the subsequent 18 years when they lived together she produced 12 children out of wedlock, before Black cast her aside in favour of a younger (married) woman. The disposed Mrs Duggan sought maintenance and in her affidavit of claim described Black (then a member of Parliament) as " ...a crafty and deep-dyed villain, a drunkard, a basher and a hot-gospelling atheist". The irate lady also affirmed that Black "told me that he did not believe in heaven; the only heaven he believed in was a woman's body".

John Norton published all this in his *Truth* and described Black, amongst other things, as "a brutal beast, an ex-pub pimp, a billiard sharper, an immoral pachyderm and a social skunk": Black promptly sued Norton but when it came to court Mr Justice Long Innes in his summing up suggested that Black's reputation was not a valuable commodity. The jury agreed and awarded Black a farthing damages without costs.

This was the man who spearheaded the campaign against Chidley the Reformer. Initially the campaign comprised constant harassment of Chidley, incessant arrests and seizure of his books, and standover tactics against the owners of halls that the Reformer had booked to air his messages. Invariably Chidley was fined and the magistrate would order that the seized copies of *The Answer* be burned.

Chidley had quite a few supporters and they invariably rallied around to pay his fines and provide him with funds to produce a new edition of *The Answer*. The ridiculous situation then arose where up one end of town the police were busily engaged in the burning of books, while down the other end of town Chidley and his supporters (with the aid of cooperative printers) were equally busy replacing them.

Finding the police campaign against Chidley bearing little fruit, "Baldy" Black deployed new tactics, having Chidley detained and charged with being insane in August 1912. He was initially held at the Reception House, before being committed to Callan Park Mental Asylum.

In doing this Black believed that the stigma of mental illness thus attached to Chidley would undermine his credence in the eyes of the public. His plan misfired badly. Fining the eccentric and peaceful Chidley was one thing, putting him in an asylum for the insane was another matter completely.

The letters column of the *Sydney Morning Herald* was filled with complaints from outraged Chidley supporters, the *Herald* even deigned to devote a minor Leader to the subject, and the matter was given a thorough airing in the Legislative Assembly. The Government did a retreat, and when the Callan Park doctors could find no evidence of Chidley's supposed insanity, he was quietly released on condition that he should cease his reform activities - a condition he totally ignored. As Chidley once said to a Magistrate who released him on the same condition: "You might as well arrest a messenger bringing tidings to a beleaguered city".

Back on the streets and in the Domain, Chidley continued his crusade, now with a lot of public support and a mantle of martyrdom.

The Labor Government of the day was in a difficult position. Claiming to be a reform government championing the underdog, it had shown itself to have been wanting in the Chidley case. They acted more circumspectly by trying to block Chidley's attempts to spread his message through public meetings. They did this by threatening to withdraw the licence of any public hall where Chidley was booked to speak, thus effectively restricting him to the weekend crowds in the Domain.

And they continued to incarcerate him for periods in Asylums on the ground that he had breached his written undertaking not to wear his Roman toga dress and to preach when he had been released from Callan Park in October 1912. It was much harder for his supporters to mount a defence to such actions when Chidley had been in clear breach of a written undertaking. However, such occasions were usually short-lived triumphs for the Government since the doctors always released him after a few months on the grounds that they could not find anything wrong with his mental health.

With the coming of World War I in 1914, the public had more important matters to think about than eccentric sex reformers, and the Chidley case gave way to war news in the papers. In the period 1914-16 Chidley was in and out of gaols and asylums more or less as officialdom saw fit. His dwindling band of supporters continued to raise funds to have him released on each occasion, but it was a losing battle in the heat of a Great War.

On September 25 1916, while at the Reception House, he penned a long "last message" to the public, pleading for a public examination of his message. A few days later he doused himself with kerosene and set fire to his clothes. Attendants quickly doused the flames and he suffered only minor burns. His flesh healed but his spirit didn't, and on December 21 1916, William James Chidley, the reformer, died at Callan Park Mental Hospital aged 56.

Perhaps his tribulations were best summed up by Havelock Ellis, when he wrote of the persecution of Chidley: "*It is sad that a new country like Australia, with so many bright prospects before it, should begin its career by setting up inquisitions*".

Finally, do you remember the foundling boy Donald ("Pad") Chidley who always believed that Chidley was his father? During World War I he enlisted in the New Zealand Expeditionary Force. In August 1916 he wrote from France to an official in Sydney asking whether there was anything he could do to help his father in his struggles with the law. The letter reached Sydney after Chidley's death. Shortly afterwards Pte DW Chidley himself was killed in action in France, never learning of his real origins or of the passing of the man he called Father.

15

The Unlucky Bullet

In an earlier chapter I referred to those seemingly innocent "hiccups of history" that can change the tide of events for a nation, for families or for individuals. One such hiccup on the other side of the globe was responsible for the arrival on Australian shores, much later and many years apart, of two unusual migrants from a family split asunder in the distant past.

The family concerned was named Laserson, originally Jewish shepherds from Spain, who in the early part of the 19th Century unwisely migrated to Konigsberg, in Germany, where both mother and father were victims of the great cholera epidemic of 1819. The Lasersons ceased to exist as a family unit as the surviving children were scattered, fostered out to family and friends in Jewish tradition of the times, losing all contact with each other.

One of the male children ended up in Mitau, the capital of the Courland Province of what is now Latvia, but then was German territory in dispute with and later occupied by Russia. When the child grew up he married and, as the Bible puts it, begat children one of whom was granted the decree of Rabbi but who did not practice as such, instead taking the path of commerce. He, in turn, begat offspring, including a male child born at Mitau on January 3 1880, who received the given name of Maurice, a child who had a remarkable career touching on the lives of the people of many lands, including Australia.

At that time Mitau was a relatively small city of some 30,000 people without secondary schooling facilities which, in any case were denied to all but a handful of the brightest Jewish scholars. Maurice Laserson fell into this category and was admitted to the Riga Polytechnic Institute. Not long after he enrolled the Russian occupying forces brought in an edict prohibiting the use of German language in schools and requiring lessons to be conducted in Russian. The pupils were not even allowed to speak with each other in German in classrooms or playgrounds, and were severely punished if caught doing so.

These restrictions did not hamper the academic progress of the young Laserson who graduated as Doctor of Commercial Science with the top honours of his class, thus automatically qualifying him for a teaching post, with the title of Professor at the Institute. There was one catch to this though. No Jew could be employed at any level in the Russian Government so to take up the coveted post he would have to renounce his Jewishness and convert to Christianity - any denomination, the authorities were not fussy on that point. Laserson point blank refused to take this step, thus condemning himself to what was the norm for Jews under the Czars - lowly , poorly paid posts in the small private sector of Russia.

As a result, in 1900 the young Maurice Laserson, entered the world of commerce in which he was later to play such a formidable role, by becoming a bookkeeper with the Westinghouse Brake Company in Petersburg. He quickly rose through the ranks and later moved to another American owned petroleum company in

Moscow with extensive interests in Grozny in the Caucasus (now capital of Chechnya), later moving to Baku working with another petroleum company based in Berlin, taking his first steps into the international arena.

The abortive Russian revolution of 1905 seems to have made a big impact on Laserson who began to take an interest in social issues and politics. To the dismay of his employers, who tried to persuade him to abandon the idea, he decided quit his high post and return to Russia to study law, and become a practising lawyer, a remarkable and extremely risky act for a Jew in those turbulent times. He was not deterred by the fact that under the rules of the day he would have to pass in Latin, a subject he had not been able to study at the Riga Polytechnic. He enrolled at Petersburg University and spent a whole year of intensive study to pass in Latin, then going on to the University's faculty of Law in Dorpat (now in Estonia) where he graduated in 1908.

The now Doctor Maurice Laserson then returned to Petersburg and set up practice as a lawyer. He was soon to find that this may have carried with it some prestige but little income. Russians could not risk the stigma then attached to having any truck with a Jew and his only clients came from the downtrodden class of fellow Jews, most of whom could not pay his fees. He was forced to accept the reality of the situation, close his practice and return to Berlin, where his old company welcomed back the prodigal.

In the succeeding years he continued his interrupted climb up the commerce ladder moving from company to company and eventually becoming Commercial Director of the Shouvalov Mining Company, a major firm with mines in the Urals and banking interests. He rode out the years of World War I this way, making some useful contacts with the Bolshevik leaders who lived in exile in Germany and Switzerland after the abortive coup of

1905.

When the 1917 Russian Revolution occurred he decided to return to Moscow and throw in his lot with the Bolsheviks - a move that his employers actually encouraged because it gave them a valuable pipeline into the new and virtually unknown group in power in Russia.

In taking this action Dr Laserson was prompted more by his heart than his head. Like many Jewish intellectuals of the time he believed the Bolsheviks when they proclaimed liberty and equality for all. He, and they, believed that a new era was about to begin for the hitherto downtrodden Jews of Russia. They had, of course, completely misread the situation. As they were to find out to their great cost a few years down the track, the Bolsheviks were as deeply anti-Semitic as the Czars. However, in the early days of the revolution this was not apparent as the Bolsheviks needed the commercial expertise, language skills and foreign contacts that the likes of Laserson possessed.

In October 1918 Dr Laserson was sent to Berlin as Financial Adviser to the Soviet Ambassador, but the posting was short-lived as the following month the German Government expelled the whole Russian Embassy.

Back in Berlin in August 1920 Laserson met up with Professor Lomonosov, then head of the Soviet Trading Mission, who offered him a job as his personal assistant. His star was on the rise and in 1923, thanks to his earlier contacts with Nicolai Krestinsky, General Secretary of the Communist Party and Peoples Commissar for Finance, Dr Laserson was offered a top ranking job in the Commissariat of Finance with the task of trying to reconstruct the shattered Russian economy.

He gained more brownie points from the Bolsheviks when he helped them sell off abroad part of the Czar's private jewel collection. For this effort he was put in charge of re-organising the shattered platinum market, of which Russia had held a monopoly prior to the war.

But rapid changes were in motion in the ranks of the Bolsheviks - none of them boding well for Dr Laserson. He left Russia for the last time on a trading mission on January 22 1924, the day that Lenin died. He was still in Berlin in 1925 when he learned that his old post in the Soviet had been abolished. The Bolsheviks, now under total control of Stalin, sought his return but his sources informed him that he was on a Stalin hit list which meant at worst a bullet in the back, and at best exile to Siberia. He wisely declined the invitation to return and severed all connections with the Soviet Union.

From 1925 to 1931 he led a relatively quiet life in Berlin, undertaking work as an economic advisor to companies, but also turning in his middle ages to painting and writing. In 1929 he wrote a major work *An Expert in the Service of the Soviet*, which was translated into English and published by Ernest Benn Ltd of London, causing quite a stir at the time as it was first account of the Russian revolution written from the inside and published in the west.

Laserson followed this up in 1931 with another book *Im Sowjet-Labyrinth*, being fairly unflattering portraits of the Soviet hierarchy. This book never did get translated into English, but it had the distinction of being banned and burned by the Nazis when they came to power in 1933, despite its anti-Soviet tone, because an inscription on the dust jacket included this comment: *Enslavement of humanity, gagging of human rights and brutal exercise of power are deeply detested by me*

But Laserson himself was not around to see the burning of his book first hand as at the end of 1931 he left Germany forever. The rise of the Nazis was the main reason but there was also a contributing factor as in that year Laserson's only child, then a student at Berlin University, was drowned while bathing at a seaside resort. Dr Laserson and his wife Hidegard without fuss quietly left Berlin and settled in Geneva where for a time he earned a meagre living writing biographical articles for newspapers and magazines on famous figures of the 20th Century, many of whom he had encountered first hand in his travels.

In 1932 he tired of this and decided to devote the rest of his life to Jewish Social Work, joining an American based welfare agency publicising the plight of German Jews being persecuted by the Nazis, and raising funds for their repatriation to less hostile parts of the world.

In the five years leading up to the outbreak of World War I Dr Laserson, who was an eloquent speaker and charismatic individual, toured the world on his rescue mission, visiting Australia on two occasions. On one of these missions, in 1938, he was to meet up with a distant cousin, also a descendant of the ill-fated Laserson family broken up by cholera in 1819. But I will come to that story later.

When World War broke out the Lasersons were virtually stranded in Geneva. When the Nazi blitzkrieg commenced in earnest in 1940, bypassing the so-called impregnable French Maginot Line, the situation seemed desperate. It was widely believed that Germany would invade Switzerland and Dr Laserson was well aware that his name was fairly high up on Nazi hit lists.

He decided to make an effort to come to Australia, but the obstacles were daunting. The only remaining route available was through France, and that seemed likely to fall to the Germans at any time. Through old contacts, he was able to get a transit visa through France and abandoning all their possessions, the couple fled, managing to reach England on one of the last boats to do so before the fall of France.

On July 2 1940 they sailed for Australia on the Orcades, first settling in Melbourne because it had a large Jewish population. But Dr Laserson quickly found that the management and technical skills he possessed were not in great demand in wartime Australia. A friend provided him with the names and addresses of 18 Jewish firms who might be able to assist, and he diligently wrote long applications to all of them. From seventeen of them he received polite notes saying there were no vacancies. From the other firm he received a letter from the managing director inviting him to an interview. But at the end of the interview there was no job offer and he inquired why, only to receive the response: "Surely you didn't really expect me to offer you a job".

When the rather bewildered Dr Laserson asked why then had he been invited to the interview, the Managing Director jovially explained: "Oh, that is simple. I just wanted to meet a man with such an amazing record".

Welcome to Australia 1940 style!

Dr Laserson wisely decided that the natives of Sydney might prove more friendly, and in this he was right, as he quickly found a niche in the Jewish community there and in June 1941 he was able to establish the World Jewish Congress (Australian Section), becoming the first Australian and New Zealand representative of the body. In the immediate postwar years he was extremely active in both the formation and operation of many Jewish bodies in Sydney, and was the honorary Australian Consul for the newly created Baltic state of Latvia. And before his death on November 26 1961, he was able to complete a major biographical work *From Russian Skies to Southern Cross - Diary of an Intellectual*, which never did make it into book format but which was published in serial format in the *Hebrew Standard* in Sydney in 1950.

With his passing, Australia lost one of its most remarkable migrants. But what of his distant cousin, that other Australian migrant from the Konigsberg tragedy of 1819? His family story is an equally amazing one.

While one Laserson male child went north to what is now Latvia, another male member of the family ended up in England where he was adopted by an English woman and sent to University. After graduating in medicine he prospered and eventually founded Tottenham hospital in London. Somewhere along the way he had a name change with the loss of the second "s" in Dr Laserson. He married and had a son, David Laseron, who is the subject of our Australian story.

David Laseron's story is unusual as he married out of the Jewish faith to an English woman, and converted to Christianity. He joined the Anglican Missionary Service and with his wife migrated to the United States, where at Manitowac, Wisconsin on December 12 1886, there was born to the couple their youngest child, Charles Francis Laseron.

The couple returned to England in 1888 and, seeking a more congenial climate, migrated to Australia three years later, settling in Sydney.

In February 1891 the Reverend David Laseron was appointed curate in charge of St George's Church, Glenmore Road, Paddington, then a quite upmarket Sydney suburb. All went well until June 4 1892 when fate, in the unlikely form of a drunken politician, dealt him a blow from which he, or his family never recovered.

Some time before that fateful day the Reverend Laseron had befriended a parishioner, a high ranking post official, George Read, (who he identified only as Mr R in his autobiography). Read had a fairly serious drinking problem which the clergyman was helping him to overcome. Read had received an invitation to attend a Postal Department picnic on the afternoon of Saturday, June 4. He was anxious to attend but knowing that beer, wine and spirits would be available at the function, decided to consult his pastor.

The Reverend Laseron was horrified at the thought of Read attending the picnic, and strongly urged him to stay away. When the weak-willed parisioner demurred, the Cleric proposed an alternative plan. He offered to have lunch with Mr Read and accompany him to Sandringham on Botany Bay for an afternoon's outing. Sandringham was at that time a popular seaside carnival area, a kind of forerunner to the later Luna Park.

Read eventually accepted the invitation and after lunch at the Coffee Palace in George Street, the pair proceeded to Central Railway Station where they boarded the steam train bound for Sandringham.

It was then that Fate played a rather dirty trick on the Reverend traveller. Initially they had taken seats opposite each other with the cleric having his back to the engine - a position he disliked. He asked his companion whether he would swap seats, and Read being agreeable, did so. This was distinctly unlucky for the Reverend Laseron as his new position proved to be the "hot spot" on the train.

Behind them was a very inebriated male passenger who, to the alarm of his fellow travellers, stood up as the train entered the subway between Everleigh and Redfern brandishing a hand pistol which he fired, probably by accident. The bullet went through the seat behind the Reverend Laseron on a downward projectory severely wounding him in the lower portion of his neck.

The culprit turned out to be Thomas Walker, aged 35, Member for Northumberland in the New South Wales Legislative Assembly.

He was an extremely controversial figure in State politics being a fierce opponent of the Premier, Sir Henry Parkes, a volatile character who was a freethinker, democrat and spiritualist and who, as a leading lecturer at Sunday gatherings, was outspoken in his denunciation of all religions. News of the train incident quickly spread, sparking instant rumours that Walker had challenged and shot the Reverend Laseron in a duel! This certainly wasn't so. He was simply drunk, not an unusual condition for him, and had been completely unaware of the presence of a member of the cloth when he started his pyrotechnical display on the train. It was certainly ironic that a mild-mannered clergyman should have been shot by someone under the influence of alcohol while on a mission to save a fellow man from the same demon!

Walker was charged with causing grievous bodily harm to the Reverend Laseron, but when he appeared in Central Criminal Court in August 1892 to answer the charge he was acquitted.

While Walker went free, the incident was to have severe and lasting consequences for the Laseron family. Two long and painful exploratory operations failed to find the bullet - there were no x-rays available in those days - and he suffered incessant pain. Little was known about the dangers of lead poisoning at that time, but it seems probable that this was the major cause of his subsequent health problems.

He suffered so much pain as a result of the presence of the bullet that he was forced to resign from the church. His parishioners rallied around and by public subscription raised enough money to send the disturbed clergyman back to England for specialist treatment and recuperation. In England the bullet was finally located and removed, some eight inches below the entry point, but by then the lead had probably poisoned his system in an irreversible manner.

He returned to Australia early in January 1896 and rejoined the church, being sent to Lithgow, first as a locum and then as Rector of St Paul's Church. He remained there for five years but his health was always poor. When he returned to Sydney he was appointed Curate of St Stephen's Church, Newtown, but ill health dogged him to such an extent that in 1902 he left the church again and commenced work with the Standard Life Association as an insurance agent.

For a time he did well in his new calling, but soon was plagued by new health and mental problems and in 1903 he was committed to the Rookwood Mental Asylum where he completed his slender work *An Autobiography - And People I have Met*, which was published by Wilson & Son, Sydney in 1904. A year later he was dead, the bullet having at last taken its toll.

His passing caused enormous problems for his family. His son, Charles Laseron, then only 19, was suddenly thrust into the role of breadwinner for his family. Charles had been a brilliant student, but all thoughts of University had to be abandoned, though he did continue private studies at Sydney Technical College and eventually became a lecturer in geology there.

In 1908, when he was 22, he joined the staff of the Sydney Technological Museum, as collector, and soon became immersed in the institution's huge collection of flora, fauna, shells, rocks and timber specimens. He was also in charge of Applied Art at the Museum and occupied that position until it was abolished in 1928.

In 1911 he joined the Mawson Expedition to Antarctica as assistant biologist , becoming a lifelong friend of Sir Douglas Mawson.

Charles Laseron served with distinction on the expedition and later wrote a book on his experiences *South With Mawson* but the manuscript lay in a London publisher's office right through the

Blitz of World War II. After the war it was retrieved by Laseron and was eventually published in Sydney in 1947 to great acclaim. It is still regarded as one of the classic pieces of writing on Antarctica.

Charles Laseron joined the first AIF on the outbreak of World War I and was a Sergeant in the 13th Battalion. He was in the original landings at Gallipoli but saw little action as he was shot in the foot on April 28 1915, and was repatriated home.

At Albury on March 22 1919 he married in the Presbyterian Church, Mary Theodora Mason, a bank clerk. They couple settled in the Blue Mountains, where their two children, a boy and a girl, were born, with Laseron commuting daily to work at the Technological Museum.

In 1919 the family moved to Manly, and with his job as head of Applied Art at the Museum, gone, he set up in business as an Antique Dealer in Hoskin Place, in the city. He was often offered stamp collections and this rekindled an earlier interest in philately so that he gradually abandoned the antique side of the business to become one of Sydney's leading stamp dealers and philatelic auctioneers. In the mid-1930's he was joined in this endeavour by his son John.

It cannot have been easy earning a living in this manner in the Great Depression years when most people had more on their minds than hobbies such as philately. Throughout this period he continued his interests in scientific matters, publishing many papers, especially in the field of conchology, in which he was an authority, and was rewarded by being made a Fellow of the Royal Zoological Society. In this period he also finished his Antarctica book and two major geology works though publication of these could not be achieved in the depression era.

My memories of him in this period are of a taciturn and very reserved individual, a man who did not suffer fools gladly, who at times had an acerbic tongue and occasionally expressed himself in a manner that caused discomfort to all in the vicinity. A certain bitterness came through in some of these "down" periods but if he was bitter, he had some justification. The bullet that laid his father low, also wrecked his own chances of what most certainly would have been a brilliant career in academia. In those far off days a F.R.Z.S. counted for little in the tight, closed circles of the Australian academic world, and there was littler recognition among his peers for his scientific papers. .

When World War II broke out Charles Laseron immediately closed his stamp shop and both he and his son John enlisted in the second AIF. Because of his age and his Gallipoli wound, he could not hope to see active service, but was a map-reading instructor, until a heart condition in 1944 forced his discharge on the grounds of medical unfitness.

He made no effort to resume his philatelic activities but for several years worked as a clerk in the Sydney office of the Colonial Sugar Refining Company.

With the publication of his pre-war manuscripts first *South With Mawson* (1947), *Face of Australia* (1953) and *Ancient Australia* (1954) there came at last the long overdue recognition of Charles Laseron's great scientific endeavours. If the recognition from Academia was somewhat muted, it was more than compensated by the public acclaim and steady sales of the works in the market place.

Charles Laseron died in the Concord Repatriation Hospital, Sydney, on June 27 1958, aged 72, after what many people would consider a full and rich life.

But how much greater would it have been, and how much richer would Australia have been, if a drunken politician had not fired that fatal shot on the afternoon of June 4 1892?

16

Drama in Antarctica

Australian history books, particularly those circulating in our schools, are full of the exploits of the early explorers, all males, who blazed trails to open up new frontiers around the continent. Yet very little attention is paid to Sir Douglas Mawson, certainly the greatest of Australia's pioneer explorers, probably because he came so late on the scene of exploration and because his endevours dealt with the frozen wastes of Antarctica.

And perhaps the average Australian knows so little about him because he was such a retiring man, a quiet academic, who does not quite fit the image of some other swashbuckling figures of the pioneering period.

Which is a pity because Mawson's achievements outshone them all, and various aspects of his action packed life have still to find their way into public print. Stories such as the way his first expedition to Antarctica came perilously close to disaster because of the actions of a mentally disturbed radio operator - a story Mawson himself was unable to tell in his book *Home of the Blizzard* (1915) because of Australia's draconian libel laws. Perhaps it is time to lift the veil on the secrecy that has to date surrounded this expedition.

But first to some background. Douglas Mawson was born in Yorkshire, England, in 1882, into a family of farmers who migrated to Australia when he was four years old. He was a star pupil at Fort Street High School in Sydney and attained a Bachelor of Science degree and later his docorate at Sydney University, where he came under the influence of the eminent geologist Edgeworth David, an influence that decided him to pursue a career in pure science.

Mawson had his field taste of field exploration in 1903 when he joined a geological expedition to the New Hebrides, producing the first geological records of these islands.

In 1905 he was appointed a lecturer in Mineralogy and Petrology at the University of Adelaide, which he served in various capacities for the rest of his life, becoming Professor of Geology and Mineralogy and head of his department in 1921.

In 1907 he had his first experience of Antarctica when he joined Ernest Shackleton's ill-fated expedition to the continent.

After being in a party of three (himself, Professor Edgeworth David, and Alistair Forbes Mackay) who were the first to climb Mt Erebus, the trio set out for the South Magnetic Pole on September 8 1908, while Shackleton and his party set out in a different direction for the South Pole. Shackleton failed in his attempt, having to turn back when they were only ninety-seven miles from their goal.

Mawson's party did succeed in reaching the Magnetic South Pole but only after suffering enormous difficulties and physical exhaustion. Edgeworth David, suffering from snow blindness, had to relinquish leadership of the party to Mawson, who managed to get them back to the ship after the longest Polar trip attempted without the aid of huskies.

Far from putting him off Antarctica for life, the experience only whet Mawson's appetite for icy adventures and in 1911 he organised his own expedition to Antarctica, chartering the whaling ship Aurora, and working in tandem with Captain Robert Scott who was to die in his attempt to conquer the South Pole.

Mawson's expedition was of a scientific nature, and succeeded in mapping over 1500 kilometres of the Antarctic coastline and gathering a enormous amount of geological and other data. But it was achieved only at a very high human cost.

After establishing a radio base at Macquarie Island, Mawson pushed on to the mainland to establish what was to become the first Australian base camp on the continent. On November 1912, Mawson left camp on what was to become one of the great epics, and also one of the great tragedies, of Antarctic exploration. He was accompanied by two sledging companions, Dr Xavier Mertz and Lieutenant Belgrave Ninnis.

The story of this journey of exploration is told by Mawson in his *Home of the Blizzard*, and in even greater detail in his diaries, published for the first time in 1988. It is a story of enormous courage and deprivation as the three men struggled against the harsh terrain and the elements - constant blizzards, even though this was summer.

The first tragedy struck on December 14, less than a month on the trail, when Ninnis fell down a crevice and was killed instantly, taking with him most of their food and other vital items - spade, tent, pick and food for the dogs. They were left with sleeping bags, a spare tent without poles and enough food for a week and a half.

Mawson and Mertz immediately turned back and had to resort to killing and eating the dogs one by one. This was to prove fatal in the case of Mertz, and almost so for Mawson, as both became seriously ill from poisoning (excessive vitamin A) as a result of eating dogs' liver. Mertz became so ill they could not travel and on January 9 1913, he died.

Mawson's position was now desperate. Starving and critically ill, his whole body was rotting from lack of proper nourishment. He had frost-bitten finger tips which were festering, the mucous membrane of his nose was gone, his saliva glands were not working and the skin was coming off his whole body. After he buried Mertz, Mawson's feet were so lumpy and sore that he decided to examine them. When he removed his socks, on the first occasion for many days, he got a great shock to find that the thickened soles of his feet had in each case separated as a complete layer with a watery fluid escaping and soaking the socks. The new skin beneath these layers was abraded and raw and his toes were black and festered near the tips. He performed makeshift surgery on his feet by smearing them with lanoline and binding the old skin layers back into place with bandages. He pulled on six layers of thick woollen sox, then fur boots and finally overshoes. The rest of his body wasn't in much better shape than the feet as the damp conditions of his sleeping bag had resulted in wholesale peeling of skin, with a number of places being rubbed raw through constant chafing. His scrotum was particularly raw and painful from the friction of walking.

At that stage Mawson recorded in his diary that there seemed little chance of his reaching the base camp. All the dogs had been slaughtered, which probably saved his life as it meant he was no longer being poisoned with excessive Vitamin D.

With no strength to pull a full sled, he cut his sled in half with a small hand saw and on January 10 he set out for the base, dragging the half-sled and his few remaining possessions and small scraps of food.

Blizzards and incessant bad weather dogged him, but a month

later, on February 8, he staggered in to the camp on Commonwealth Bay to find the *Aurora* had sailed a few hours earlier, have delayed its departure as long as possible but being forced to leave for fear of being trapped in the pack ice. The parallels to the experience of Burke & Wills when on the afternoon of April 21 1861 they staggered into their base camp at Coopers Creek only to find the message at the "Dig Tree" that their relief party had departed only that morning are uncanny. Burke & Wills died of starvation as a result.

Mawson was luckier as his second in charge Captain Davis had left behind to winter over at the huts a small relief party hoping against hope that Mawson, Mertz and Ninnis would turn up.

By this time Mawson was in a desperate state, having lost almost half his body weight, which had dropped from 95 kilos to 51 kilos and being in urgent need of medical help. The relief team could not make direct contact with the Aurora but was able to get a message through to it via the Macquarie Island radio base advising Captain Davis of the death of Mertz and Ninnis and of the plight of Mawson.

Captain Davis immediately turned the Aurora around and attempted to get back to the base the next day, but the pack ice was moving in and he had to abandon the attempt, though the base team could see the ship in the far distance.

There was nothing for it but for Mawson and the relief team to stay over for another entire bitter Antarctic winter until they could be relieved at the end of 1913.

Mawson subsequently wrote that his experience in sinking to the lowest depths of starvation without perishing had so disorganised his system that it was two months before he could sleep properly or do anything but eat and doze with frequent interruptions from internal disorders.

It was in this period that he sent off a message to his fiancee, Francisca Adriana (Paquita) Delprat, daughter of Guillaume Daniel Delprat (then Manager of Broken Hill Pty Ltd): *"Deeply regret delay stop only just managed to reach hut stop effects now gone but lost most of my hair stop you are free to consider your contract but trust you will not abandon your second hand Douglas."*

The couple were married a year later.

But first Mawson and his party had to survive the severe Antarctica winter in a small (mostly) galvanised iron hut. And for this they had to survive problems other than blizzards and extremes of temperature.

They had a pretty formidable human problem on their hands. The relief party of six that Captain Davis left behind comprised Francis Bickerton, Robert Bage, Cecil Madigan, Dr Archie McLean, Alfred Hodgeman and Sidney Jeffries.

The odd man out, in all senses of the word, was the last named Sidney Jeffries, who was not really a member of Mawson's team, as were the other five, but was the Radio Operator on the *Aurora*. Captain Davis had decided the group might need a fully qualified Radio Operator. Bickerton could receive and slowly transmit but was not qualified.

Mawson's heart must have sank when he sighted Jeffries who was no stranger to him. Back in 1911 when he was forming his team, Jeffries had applied for the post of Radio Operator, but Mawson, who was a good judge of character immediately spotted him as a "wrong 'un" and rejected his application, despite Jeffries' paper qualifications. The 1912 team replacements were left to Captain Davis, as deputy leader. When Jeffries applied to him for the position of ship's Radio Operator, he made no mention of his former application to and rejection by Mawson.

The realty was that Jeffries was mentally unstable, a fact that put the whole operation in Antarctica in that terrible winter of 1913 at considerable risk, problems that Mawson could well have done without considering his fragile health at the time.

In his *Home of the Blizzard*, Mawson made only passing reference to "problems with the Radio Operator". As Jeffries was still very much alive, he could hardly have done otherwise, given Australia's draconian laws.

More than three quarters of a century would elapse before the truth would emerge with the publication of Mawson's private diaries in 1988 - diaries which were highly personal and which Mawson never thought would be given public scrutiny.

The extent of the problem may be gauged by the fact that there are eighty three references to Jeffries scattered through the diaries, almost all of them unfavourable, and many clearly indicating the frustration and anger which boiled up in Mawson in his daily efforts to cope with the very unstable personality under his control.

The problems were on several fronts, ranging from the minor but unpleasant one experienced on a daily basis by Jeffries' lack of personal hygiene, his refusal to wash his clothes or to take a bath - this in the very close confines of a blizzard bound hut with seven adults crowded together. On one occasion when Jeffries was persuaded to take a bath , Mawson sardonically noted that the other members were of the opinion that the canvas bath they used would have to be disinfected!

Another running sore throughout the winter was the refusal of Jeffries to do the domestic chores of cooking, washing up and cleaning which all members did on a roster basis. Even when forced to do something, he did it in such a slovenly manner that someone else had to go along and pick up the pieces.

He was very belligerent to all the other team members, occasionally to Mawson, and on several occasions provoked or attempted to provoke physical clashes. There are other cryptic entries by Mawson that cry out for more detail, such as the one that simply said "Jeffries sat in butter pudding".

Such incidents might be passed off as being caused by the close confines of a hut in Antarctica, or to personality clashes between incompatible individuals. By far the bulk of Mawson's complaints centred on Jeffries duties as Radio Operator and to his neglect of these duties to an extraordinary degree.

Radio reception was best at night, preferably after midnight but working to this schedule was not to Jeffries inclination despite the fact that he undertook no domestic chores or rarely ventured outside in the brief spells of good weather, as did the others. He spent most of his days sulking in his bunk, dozing or reading, getting up only for meals. Then most evenings he refused to do any radio work after ten o'clock.

He refused to show Mawson what he was transmitting and Mawson suspected, correctly as it turned out, that Jeffries was not transmitting the official reports he was given, but personal messages. Bickerton occasionally took over and transmitted (slowly) some reports, but even this alternative was closed on occasions when Jeffries removed crystals or other working parts from the set thus putting it out of action so that Bickerton could not use it. It was a very dangerous situation that could have had serious consequences had a real emergency occurred.

The situation became so bad that on September 2 Mawson had Bickerton transmit a message to the Macquarie Island Station stating that Jeffries was insane. In his diary notes, Mawson on several occasions noted that it was his opinion that Jeffries was a certifiable case. And the thought must always have been at the back of the minds of the others that Jeffries might go over the edge and run amok with a meat cleaver or some other object. In the end

Mawson had to devise a secret roster whereby one of the six always had to keep Jeffries under observation.

Living in closely confined conditions on a ship or the mainland would be extremely difficult; having to live them in a small iron hut in Antarctica where blizzards made escape outside impossible most of the time must have been an extremely nerve wracking experience for all except the cause of their problems - their so-called Radio Operator. And it must have been of enormous relief to all when the *Aurora* entered the bay and anchored on the morning of December 13 1913.

For Mawson the long journey was nearly over. He returned to Australia on the *Aurora* at the end of that summer in 1914 to a hero's welcome, a Knighthood, and honours from the world scientific community, and for a long and fruitful marriage to the girl of his dreams. The only sour note came from a mean-minded Federal Government which declined to help him pay off the debt of five thousand pounds which the expedition had accumulated because of the stay over of the extra winter in Antarctica. This debt he paid off over the years out of his University salary.

Apart from a spell of war service, he spent the rest of his life in academia but always retained his interest in the Antarctic continent. In 1929 and 1931 he led scientific summer cruises to Antarctic conducting aerial surveys and marine studies, and it was mainly due to him that in 1933 Great Britain ceded to Australia a major part of its claims to the continent. He was also instrumental in the establishment of the first Australian National Antarctic Expedition in 1947 and Australia's main base on the continent is named Mawson after him.

Mawson died on October 14 1958 following a cerebral haemorrhage and was awarded a Commonwealth State funeral, bringing to a close a remarkable life of courage, determination and achievement against all the odds.

But what of his nemesis, the radio operator Sidney Jeffries who caused him such problems and heartache in that terrible winter of 1913.

Jeffries also returned to Australia on the Aurora at the end of the summer of 1914 and was committed to a mental asylum at Ararat, Victoria. How long he stayed in that institution I do not know as I have not been able to find any records relating to him after 1914.

However, I do have in my philatelic collection of Antarctic material two items relating to Jeffries, one of which throws a lot of light on his state of mind when he returned from Antarctica.

These came into my possession in unusual circumstances. I was at a week long National Philatelic Exhibition (ANPEX) in Sydney in 1970 when I was approached by a very elderly woman, whose age I guessed was over eighty. She had been told by two dealers at the Exhibition that I was a collector of Antarctic material and might be interested in two items she wished to sell. My field was postal history of the Antarctic continent, and these did not fall into that category, being more in the class of ephemera. Still, even ephemera items from Antarctic are not common and they did add interest to a collection so we agreed on a price and we parted company. I gained the distinct impression that because of her advanced age she was not interested in the monetary side of the transaction so much as wanting to find a safe home for a couple of items which had for her treasured memories of the time some sixty years before when she had briefly befriended a young man named Jeffries then about to depart for Antarctica.

At that time the name Jeffries meant nothing to me, as I did not know of the trials and tribulations that Mawson had had with his radio operator, so I made no attempt to extract from the lady any background information about the items. She did not volunteer her married name or her address, so I was unable to make contact when I returned home and studied the items carefully realising for the first time that I might have an interesting piece of Antarctic history in my possession.

The first item, which initially attracted my attention, was a telegram which Jeffries sent the woman from Adelieland to her Randwick address. It was probably sent by morse code by Jeffries on the evening of April 13 1913 to the Expedition Radio station on Macquarie Island. The island operator transmitted it to Hobart which in turn sent it on to Sydney, where it was sent out to Randwick for delivery. The message was brief and of no special significance : "KIND MESSAGE MUCH APPRECIATED - JEFFRIES". The Randwick postmark is of April 14 1913.

This was a period when Douglas Mawson was recovering from his ordeal and was seriously disoriented, both mentally and physically. In the two months that followed his return to the Base Camp on Commonwealth Bay, he tried to maintain his daily diary, but his entries were very brief, and usually only comprised a weather note. On April 13 and 14 a blizzard was raging outside so the men were confined to the hut. There was no mention of Jeffries at all in the diaries in this period, as many weeks were to elapse before Mawson gained sufficient strength to take over the leadership role. And that was when Jeffries started to go over the edge.

The second of my acquisitions proved to be much more interesting in the historical sense since it was an eight page letter which Jeffries wrote to the woman from the Ararat Asylum, on July 14 1914 only a few short months after his committal. It certainly throws a lot of light on Jeffries' mental state at the time and, since such serious allegations were levelled against him by Mawson and (apparently) his companions in Antarctica, fairness dictates that we should hear his side. It is presented below in its entirety , the first time that Jeffries version of events in the winter of 1913 has been published:

Ararat.
July 14th.

Dear Miss Eckford,

It was not my purpose to write to any of my friends, but Mrs Fox informed me that you were enquiring as to my illness, & seemed concerned.

My lifelong friends do not believe my case is as I state, & imagine I have delusions. Knowing how difficult it is, on the evidences they have; to come to any other conclusions; I have not endeavoured to elucidate matters. I do not expect to be more successful in your case either, but after telling you the absolute Truth, I leave it entirely to your own discretion to say whether it is Truth or delusions.

When I tell you that my reason, memory, and all my faculties of mind are as good as ever they were; and yet I am insane it will seem paradoxical, but it is really so. The newspaper reports of my case were entirely erroneous. I am not keen that the public should know the actual case, for should the Angel Gabriel come to earth & tell the story, he would not be believed. Personally I care nothing for public opinion, otherwise I might have sought to gain it. When the press reporter at Stawell interviewed me, I told him I preferred not to be interrogated by the press and pander to the curiosity of an all too morbid public. It would take a volume to go into the details of that year, and I can only tell you the principal occurrences which led up to my present condition. If I should use the personal pronoun too often, overlook it, as I can hardly explain my case otherwise. I left Sydney anxious to succeed and as I think I remarked to you, caring little what happened, if only I made good.

Once away from Australia I entered into the spirit of the thing with zest. I assure you that after reaching the Antarctic after an interesting trip through the pack ice, I gladly accepted the offer to form one of the relief party selected to search for Mawson & his comrades. The very afternoon the ship left, Mawson returned minus his comrades. I recalled the ship by wireless at Mawson's request. The Aurora returned, but owing to a blizzard coming on meanwhile, Capt Davis decided to leave us for another year, & pick up Frank Wilds party; whom he had landed on the barrier some twelve months previous; & for whom he had some apprehensions regarding their safety. Mawson & myself seemed the only ones who cared about spending a year there. They all had already been some fourteen months in the Antarctic when I came down, & were thoroughly homesick; However, all went well for some months. I made the keeping up of the wireless mast my chief objective. Mawson and the others considered it an impossibility, and no attempt had been made the previous year. This did not deter me however, and I was succeeding fairly well, & it seemed likely that I could manage to make it weather the entire winter.

The blizzards kept increasing, and blew for weeks together at a speed of 80 to 100 miles per hour. The wind rarely ceased for more than a day or so & even in the midsummer months a calm day was rare.

When it seemed apparent that the mast was going to weather the storms, a wave of jealousy swept over the other six members. Having no experience in these matters, I never for a moment dreamt that it would lead to the insanity and although I noticed it, I never stopped my efforts. Evidences of something wrong first appeared in Madigan & McLean who continually gave vent to cowardly insinuations. I stood a good deal of this without demur, but got into open conflict with Dr McLean first. We shook hands but Madigan made a scurrilous insinuation against Mawson, with regard to Mertz, & in taking Mawson's part, I then got into trouble with Madigan. I became the central point of attack by all except Mawson & Hodgeman. Things were getting very warm when suddenly the mast came down. Seeing the jealousy that had arisen, Mawson should not have wished me to try to erect it in the face of such opposition. In trying to push the work on in accordance with Mawson's suggestion, I unhinged what remaining good was left in the others, and they used all the arts within their compass to drive me from the hut and at the same time to protect themselves. Mawson & Hodgeman joined the other four, and although Mawson pretended to be assisting me, he was no better than the rest. Insinuations of the most odious kind were made against me, & they endeavoured to break down my nerves by keeping me awake at night, and trying to get me to leave the hut. I now had nothing left to do, but endure all as best I could. Mawson & Hodgeman probably imagining that I would weather the business, & turn evidence, or being themselves weather-made, & jealousy obsessed, suddenly changed round and succeeded in a measure in gaining my confidence They then made every effort to hypnotise me, although I could not make out what they were up to at that time, having no knowledge whatever of occult sciences. The result was, that I again fell a victim to what proved worse than damnation. After a few of their hypnotic endeavours, which I misunderstood then, I woke one morning feeling a strange calmness, and with a queer feeling of strength of nerves. I immediately repaired to Mawson & asked him if I could assist in any way in keeping order. He said, Oh you slept well, did you. Go & have a lie down,

He immediately dressed & resorted to attracting & trying to fix my attention. I could not understand his attitude, but I shortly after fell into a magnetic spell My will & all my faculties remained exactly as they were before, and the change which I actually felt traverse my brain & which it seemed to strengthen, exposed my thoughts & feelings to all & sundry in the hut. The fact is, that my will became suddenly magnetic and I am in a permanent state of mental thought transference, telepathy or whatever you chose to call it. This is what people cannot bring themselves to believe, a consider a delusion. They can easily assure themselves of its reality by writing to the Supt of this bug-house & I wager them all, he will not refute it. To continue with the tragedy. I then kept order as well as I could by this means of thought transference, deciding to pilot them home without bloodshed if possible, & get out of the way before the ship reached Adelaide. This I did as anyone who came down on the ship can certify. A week before arriving at Adelaide I took an overdose of opium but although I took enough to dispose of any 2 men it never so much as made me feel drowsy. I decided to go on to Australia & try more natural methods & left the train at Stawell with a determination to starve to death. "A la suffragette eh",? Well, although I had twelve days without a bite, I felt little the worse for it, and was not roaming the bush as people may imagine, but calmly awaiting the end (in one spot) which seemed so hard to reach. Some Lady it appears wrote to the Law Authorities knowing I was starving myself, according to evidence put forward, and I refused to give any information or explanation to the Law, except that I had been to the Antarctic & I blamed Dr Mawson's hypnotism as being the chief instrument in bringing about my mental condition, although it was only one factor. How the Lady in question got the information I cannot say, as I know no one was told of my whereabouts or intentions. My condition does not appear to have mended in the least since the day the change over me in the Antarctic, and is more serious & far reaching than any of my friends imagine. The other six members escaped the fate of an asylum but I guess they still have the mania for "notoriety at any cost whatever" which afflicted them right up till their arrival in Australia.

I want it clearly understood that you must not reply to this. Whether you believe in it or otherwise rests entirely with yourself & your capacity for believing truths which seem incredible & yet are not so. These men were unfortunate in not being able to control their jealousies. and had conditions more trying probably than any other expedition ever experienced. We must not judge them, lest we be judged ourselves. I leave them to God & their own consciences

Take good care of Mrs Fox, & pardon the length of this epistle, I leave you to cogitate on what you have here, and close with assurances of my kind regards to yourself & sister.

Yrs sincerely Sidney Jeffries.

PS. Keep this information strictly confidential. I do not want it to become newspaper controversy, but I have given most of my friends whose intimacy I have valued similar reports, & I have enough confidence in you to know you will keep this as much to yourself as possible. The matter is public enough here, but I would hate to have it spread. I have stopped all correspondence, except with members of my own family. I won it be able to come up to the scratch for that skating challenge I threw out before I left for the Antarctic; anyhow, most of our skating down there consisted of slipping about the ice infinnesko, with following winds at 80 to 100 miles either behind or in front. Suppose you still patronise the ice rink. My days of joy rides etc seem to have ended, when I shall regain a normal condition is beyond me to say, and I don't altogether see how they can keep me locked up here. I'm optimistic enough as a rule, but I long for a dissolution of mind & body. I have not the slightest fear of death & would welcome it as my best friend. A strange fate to have befallen me. Hope this letter won't make you bluey. Goodbye. Excuse the smudges. I'm writing under rather unusual conditions. I hope no other of your acquaintances will ever haul up at a rat-house. I feel this really more on their account, than on my own. I have made martyrs of my own family & yet I could not have avoided it. It was to be. sounds like the Mohammedan's Kismet, doesn't it. I almost forgot to thank you for your wireless message. Suppose you received my reply from Antarctic. Several of our private msgs were not forwarded from the Hobart end I have since learnt.

Ed Note: The Mawson diaries erroneously spell Jeffries given name as "Sydney".

17

Our Politicians

I understand what truth and democracy is and I don't put my knee on the same altar as politicians.

Nice quotation, but who said it?

Actually it was Bob Hawke away back in 1973 when he was President of the ACTU long before he became a politician. And we all know what happened to him, don't we?

But he was right in the beginning. In Australia politicians enjoy a status about on par with an Army field latrine, and complaints about their standard goes right back to the last century. Francis W.Adams in his "Australian Essays" of 1886, for instance noted:

"Political life at present in Europe can scarcely be called noble, but here in Australia it is positively so base that there is a danger of it becoming a monopoly of men whose verbose incompetence is only equalled by their jovial corruption." Almost a hundred years on, John Pringle, when he came here from England to be Editor of the *Sydney Morning Herald* was soon to comment: "No country deserves politicians as bad as these."

O.K. we have got the message, but why is this so?

A lot has to do with the history of our young nation since white settlement in 1788. For the first six decades Australia was merely a convenient convict dumping ground of the British Empire, run from Whitehall as a series of far-away garrisons.It was, quite bluntly, run on the lines of a military dictatorship with very little concessions to democracy extended even to the ever-growing numbers of free settlers. It was not until more than half a century had passed that the vast island continent started to be carved up into self-governing colonies and given some token measures of parliamentary forms.

This stage of our development more or less coincided with the discovery of gold when it became a case of every man for himself in the rush to be rich. And there were indeed rich pickings for anyone with energy and imagination, if not from the nuggets in the ground, then from meeting the needs of our vastly expanding population. In short there were better, and more profitable, things to do than to enter politics where financial rewards were either absent or meagre. Only the second-raters adopted politics as a career path. The majority concentrated on getting rich.

So, with some honourable exceptions, we got a standard of politician in the state parliaments that we did not deserve. One of the most disreputable of was John Norton, the controversial owner of the scandal sheet "Truth", a an alcoholic blackmailer, wife-beater, and man of violence. In 1901 in his own paper, he described a sitting of the NSW Legislative Assembly, of which he was a member, as follows:

"Members sit, with bloodshot eyes, foul breath and disordered clothing, alternately leering at the galleries and swearing at each other. At last, late at night, they resolve to return home. They stagger down the steps, nearly breaking their 'respectable' necks in the process and fall in heaps on the Macquarie Street pavement.

Staggering to their feet, some of them proceed to bargain with and swear at the cabmen it would not surprise 'Truth to learn that they had slept off, in a brothel, the effects of their potations".

From its very beginning in the mid-19th Century our Parliamentary democracy has thrown up a remarkable collection of characters (all male) with some way out ideas and behaviour. And there is no better example of this than a member of the very first freely elected Australian Parliament, the New South Wales Legislative Assembly of 1858.

The member concerned was Bourn Russell, a former sea captain who in the early 1830's was in command of the Lady Rowena, a ship of some 350 tons especially fitted out by its English owners for trading around the South Pacific and Asian ports. On its maiden voyage as a trader under the command of Captain Russell it covered a considerable territory in more than two years of meandering around the Pacific and Orient. And we know a lot about this voyage, and the attitudes of its rather eccentric captain, because its extensive log from its departure from Sydney in May 1830, to its return there in June 1832, is held on loan in the archives of the Sydney Mitchell Library. And quite an extraordinary log it is too, since Captain Russell was a well educated man with some literary style and filled his log with acute and interesting observations on the people and places he visited, as well as charting a considerable number of previously unexplored waters, including all the Solomon Islands. The voyage was not without incident, and perhaps the best example of Captain Russell's outlook and actions can be found in his description of his encounter with the natives of what he called *Niphon* (i. e. the place we now call Japan). The methods he used to befriend the locals were, to say the least, unique, even by the standards of his time.

Captain Russell arrived in Japanese waters in April 1831, being desperately short of wood and water, and other fresh food supplies. To remedy this situation he anchored in a large bay, which he named Rowena Bay, approximately a hundred miles south of the capital Jeddo (now called Tokyo). Around the shores of the bay were several villages of poor farmers and fishermen, and he centred his attention on the largest of these settlements, a village of several hundred inhabitants perched on a ridge. This small village, named Agitana, was to be the scene of much action in the next few days.

The captain's plan was to go ashore, accompanied by a small but heavily armed force from his crew, and open up trading negotiations with the natives, as he had successfully done in the various islands. But his plan misfired seriously when the villagers fled into the bush behind the village as soon as they sighted his force approaching. Some of the men later returned and took up positions in several small forts at one end of the village and resisted all attempts by Captain Russell to persuade them to come out and talk. Instead they preferred to throw spears and rocks at his forces when they approached the forts. After several days of this Mexican stand-off the natives, apparently having run out of spears and rocks, abandoned their forts and went bush again, leaving behind only one native which the Captain had been able to capture.

Captain Russell was quite furious at his failure to open up trade relations with the good citizens of Agitana, failing entirely to appreciate the fact that the locals had taken to their heels because they feared being shot and that they didn't have the faintest idea what the Captain was talking about when he shouted at them because the two parties had no common means of communication. So Captain Russell did what any full blooded Englishman would have done in the circumstances: he burned the whole village to the ground. This was no difficult task as the fragile houses were only built of wood with thatched roofs.

Having accomplished this the by now very furious captain took his solitary prisoner back to the Lady Rowena and sat down and wrote a fiery letter of protest to the Emperor of Japan surely one of the most unusual and explosive diplomatic documents of history in this part of the world. Fortunately for posterity, Captain Russell was a meticulous man, he made a copy of his letter in his Log, before entrusting the original to his prisoner of war, with explicit instructions to hasten to Jeddo and deliver it personally to the Emperor. Whether the unfortunate fellow understood these instructions and actually carried them out is a moot point, as history is silent on whether the Emperor ever received the missive, had it translated or responded in any way to it. At this late stage, all we can do is sit back and marvel at the actual wording of the document.

The letter carried the dateline of Agitana, April 15 1831, and was addressed to His Most Celestial Highness The Emperor Of Japan and the text was as follows:

I came to the village of Agitana and saw your people; we were their friends; your subjects the Japanese persuaded the Tartars (i e. Chinese) we were enemies and everyone ran to Agitana and made forts to fight us; this was not our object; we only wanted wood and water; and shelter from bad weather to repair our ship; which we willingly would have paid for. And as they were so inhospitable as not to supply us; but show fight after waiting many days, I chastised them for their perverseness by fighting them although ten times our number! We took one Japanese prisoner and their flags and the rest ran away.

And for presuming to fire on a stranger instead of supplying his wants I burnt their village and took what I wanted, but I spared, out of compassion, all the villages where they did not fight, except one house burnt by accident. I hope all my countrymen will do the same, burn and destroy all your towns and villages that refuse the hospitality which is due to every man; which they are well able to do even your city of Jeddo (Tokyo) until you order that they may enter any of your ports and be supplied with such refreshments as they want, and they will pay for all they get; and should it be mutually advantageous to Trade, you must allow your subjects to do so; and you will soon be convinced that Europeans are not Monsters, but that they are infinitely further advanced in the Arts and Sciences and Civilisation than you are; of which fact you can scarcely. (I think) be ignorant; And in the Art of War you can judge from the encounter at Agitana, that you quite in the Darkness - England can produce 120 000 soldiers, equal in fine discipline to twice the number of us who fought you at Agitana; and be assured that the Wars of Europe have spared you from being chastised for the many insults you have offered to Europeans.

The English by their own Laws are bound to respect the laws of Other Countries while in them and always consider themselves amenable to these Laws so far as Justice and Equity direct them; so that you need not fear to have either your Laws or your Religion subverted; unless you think ours better; but do not suppose we are so ignorant as these Spanish and Portuguese Priests whom you murdered many years ago. This is another and more enlightened age with us.

I have no doubt but the Dutch whom you permit to Trade with you at Nangasaski (Nagasaki) endeavour to keep you as ignorant of European affairs as much as we know *you* keep them in *subjection*, but be not deceived; Englishmen will never degrade themselves by some of your Ceremonies but they will show True Respect after the manner of their own country.

Should you not concede to the request of this letter beware of ill-treating Englishmen in enticing them on shore to make them Prisoners which we know has been done in some cases; but if any fall into your hands keep treating them as I have done the Prisoner whom I now liberate to convey this letter - or your known villages and ships shall suffer for it.

Your good intentions can be easily made known to the English Government by the Dutch, Thro' China or. be sent on board an English ship on your coast by a Fisherman.

With all the Respect you may conceive to be due to you without degrading formalities, I am your obedient servant - an Englishman.

The letter was peppered throughout with Chinese characters (the meaning of which eluded Captain Russell), plus drawings of the English Flag and the captured Japanese flag. In a footnote in the Log, Captain Russell explained his reason for doing this: "The Language of this letter was chosen as being little liable to be translated erroneously and the Chinese characters, and the Flags, were inserted as connecting links that would not be misunderstood and they may also incite curiosity to have the whole translated. They will also be a check upon Dutch translation."

Having fired off this missive to the Emperor , Captain Russell departed from Japanese waters seeking fresh fields to conquer. Four years later, in 1835, he quit the sea permanently to settle in Australia. He opened a general store in West Maitland, New South Wales, which appears to have been a successful venture as in time he became a substantial landholder in the Maitland district.

In 1856 when the first Parliamentary election was held in Australia, for the New South Wales Legislative Assembly, he successfully stood as a candidate in the Northumberland Boroughs, being sworn in on March 28, as one of the small group of freely elected parliamentarians. His stay in the Legislative Assembly was brief as on August 5, the same year he resigned to become a life member of the Upper House, the Legislative Council. And there he remained until his death on July 4 1880.

Over the years many politicians have committed criminal acts of one kind or another, but only a percentage of such villains have ended up behind bars. This is because many of their criminal acts have been in the field of corporate misdeeds, always hard to prosecute. But again the numbers of such crimes have been minute compared to the total number of politicians scattered through our state and federal parliaments since the 1850's. There is one however, who deserves to be put in a class all his own because he is the only known murderer to have served in both the NSW Legislative Assembly and Federal Parliament. This Thomas John Ley (1879-1947) who was born in England and brought to Australia as a child. He founded the Sydney legal firm of Ley, Andrews & Co, and was elected to NSW Parliament in 1917, serving as Minister for Justice from 1922-25. In 1925 he resigned to contest the Federal seat of Barton which he won, after a bitter contest in which his Labor opponent Frederick Albert McDonald accused Ley of attempting to bribe him. Shortly after the election McDonald disappeared after leaving to attend an appointment with Ley, and it is believed that Ley was responsible for his disappearance (and probably his murder) Ley was soon embroiled in fraud charges of a serious nature and two men involved in bringing charges against him met sticky ends. One Hyman Goldstein, a member of the NSW Parliament, was found dead at the foot of Coogee cliffs, and the other, Kenneth Greedor, disappeared in mysterious circumstances. Ley was defeated in the 1928 election as a result of the ensuing scandal, and hastily left for England where he engaged in a series of dubious enterprises, and in World War II was active in various black market undertakings.

In November 1946 the body of a man, John Bain Mudie, was found in a chalkpit in Surrey. Ley and an accomplice Lawrence John Smith were charged and found guilty of the murder of Mudie.

Both were sentenced to death but on appeal Smith was given a life sentence and Ley was declared insane and sent to Broadmoor Lunatic Asylum where he died on July 24, 1947. Ley probably murdered (or arranged the murder) of four men, including a fellow politician! Ley incidentally was a teetotaller who campaigned strongly against the evils of the demon grog, and who made many enemies in and out of Parliament with his sectarian crusades. Voters do elect some strange types to parliament, don't they?

I would like to end this chapter with a Political Quiz:

Give the year of publication of the first press coverage of an Australian political meeting, real or imagined?

As it is unlikely you will come up with the answer I will provide it immediately: The year was 1786.

Hang on a minute the First Fleet didn't arrive in Botany Bay until 1788 - how could there be a political meeting in 1786?

The answer is that for several years before the departure of the Fleet for Botany Bay there was considerable coverage of the expedition in the British (and Irish) press and 1786 Walker's Hibernian Magazine in Dublin came up with a quite account/ political delightful imaginary events to come in this strange new land in the antipodes. As there were no buildings to house the parliament, the magazine used its imagination and set the meeting in a tree with a speaker sitting on a bough and members and public crowded around the trunk. The woodcut of this historic event carried the caption *The first Parliament of Botany Bay in high debate*. The article that followed was headed *Botany Bay- House Of Assembly. A Hasty Sketch of yesterday's debate*. Then followed text of the debate as follows:

The Speaker having taken the tree, Mr Ketch, Secretary To The Executions, produced several papers - which had been called for on the proceeding day of meeting; from which it appeared that thirteen colonists had been hanged for murder.

He then moved the assembly, that the sum of six shillings and eight pence be voted to reimburse the state for the expense of halters.

Father Luke objected on principles of economy, and entered to a long and learned argument to shew that notwithstanding the stretching quality of ropes, one halter, if used with caution, serve for several executions, and it was the more necessary to be economic in this article as the insurgents of the last year had destroyed the hempen plantations and burned down the rope manufactory; and also because it was probable that when the next fleet of transports arrived from England, the demand for halters would increase considerably - he therefore moved that the question be postponed till the day appointed for the consideration of the civil list establishment.

On the question being put, it was ordered accordingly.

18

The Beauteous Terrorist

Today's crop of State Premiers are a pretty colourless bunch compared to some of the figures who strutted across the political scene in the last century.

Our present Premiers are surrounded by "Minders" who get apoplexy if their charges step out of lines of political correctness even marginally. Imagine their reaction if some modern Premier took it into his head to write and self-publish a book of execrable poetry, some about clearly identified mistresses, all topped up by a an epic poem and dedicating the book itself to a Russian Terrorist?

But then modern Premiers aren't made in the mould of Sir Henry Parkes, five times Premier of New South Wales, and a bit a law unto himself, especially when it involved handsome women.

Henry Parkes (1815-1896) was born in Warwickshire, England, and migrated to Australia in 1839 with his first wife (he married three times, on the last occasion, in his dotage, to a sprightly 23-year-old). Having had no formal education, he worked first as a farm hand, then as a Customs Officer in Sydney until he set up shop as an ivory and bone turner.

In 1850 he founded the Empire newspaper, which was an influential organ until it failed with debts of fifty thousand pounds. In 1854 he was elected to the New South Wales Legislative Council and for the next forty years was in and out of politics like a Jack-in-the-box, representing various constituencies and serving five terms as premier. Although an able politician and a skilled orator, he was hopeless at managing his financial affairs and died in poverty in 1896. He had been awarded the KCNG in 1877 and the GCMG in 1888.

Sir Henry was always a soft touch where the ladies were concerned, and he seems to have got quite carried away when he read the story of an 18th Century Russian beauty named Sophia Perovskaia, who belonged to the aristocracy, but who renounced her heritage to]oin the outlawed Terrorist Party. She was betrayed, captured and hanged by the Czar's minions.

Moved greatly by the story, Sir Henry sat down and penned the following epic to the now long-departed Sophia:

Soft as the morning's pearly light, Where yet may rise the thunder-cloud,
Her gentle face was ever bright With noble thought and purpose proud.
Dreamt ye that those divine blue eyes, That beauty free from pride or blame,
Were fashion'd but to terrorize O'er Despot's power of sword and flame?
Beware! Those beauteous lineaments Of girlhood shrine a force sublime,
Which moulds to fearful use events, And dares arraign Imperial crime.
A fear was in the peasants' eyes, A palsy smote both tongue and hand;
A network of police and spies O'erspread the tyrant-tortured land.
The dungeons swallowed all our best who next would perish none could say;

A thousand victims of arrest Were torn from us one summer day.
The Judges, sworn to guard the right,, Interpreted the tyrant's bent;
Though cleared by witnesses of light 'Twas hard to save the innocent.
The Senate, in its ordered state, Might free - its voice inspired no awe;
Acquittal did not liberate The Autocrat annulled the law.
The tender, sweet Enthusiast,
The bright-eyed maid with hero's soul, Had watched the thickening shadow cast
O'er all the land, in death and dole.
Her girlhood's secret studies, late And early, in her princely home;
Her converse with the good and great, The lessons taught by Greece and Rome,
Had nerved her heart to action strong; She joined the few who dared the worst,
Resolved the strike the monster Wrong To wrestle with the Thing accurst!
Pale Freedom's devotees, whose creed Was vengeance, who in silent trust
Prepared themselves to bear and bleed And bravely die - if die they must.
what matter 'd, so the Despot's doom, And Freedom's advent, nearer drew?
Their chosen path was through the gloom The peril of their choice they knew.
To give their all, even life, were sweet Not half, as Ananias gave -
So they might see the work complete, Or feel it finished in the grave.
The early rose of womanhood
Had scarcely ill turned her angel face, When mongst conspirators she stood -
The bravest in the darkest place.
In danger, failure, suffering, she Cheer'd on with her unchanging smile,
Still looking forth to victory, As free from doubt as far from guile.
Stern men pursued the work of death No war-cry raised, no flag unfurled They laid the mine whose nitric breath

Should blow the tyrant from the world.
Dark warfare! - oh, how pitiless! What else for them? - no right of speech,
No right of meeting for redress, No right the rights of man to teach!
How plead their cause in burning words? How arm 'd in just rebellion rise -
where gleam a million servile swords, where prowl for prey a million spies.
To counsel, organize, sustain, To plan escape, to lead attack,
Her steady hand and luminous brain Were ever Onward - never Back!
Her voice was like a holy bell, Calling to highest sacrifice;
When black disaster heaviest fell, She stood all smiles to pay the price!
Baffled surprise and bold escape, Endurance long, at last are o'er;
The Monster's jaws insatiate gape. whose cry for blood is ever More!
The hunters close around her path, Her forfeit life is in their hands;
She neither bends before their wrath, Nor braves her captor's hireling bands.
She meets her fate serene and still, Above all earthly hopes and fears;
If once her eyes the teardrops fill, Her mother's grief unlocks the tears.
The mockery of trial came,
And follow'd swift the words of doom; But ignominy, woe, and shame
Were far from her - her dungeon tomb
Held spiritual companions, there
A light, which others could not see, Shone in her heart, and everywhere To die was only to be free!
Six days no friendly face came near, No sister's clinging arm, no word
From all the loved ones reach'd her ear Her mother's voice no more was heard.
Six days the weeping mother sought To see her sentenced child in vain;
Their eyes ne'er met till she was brought rth in the daylight - to be slain
She stood beneath the felon rope Her beauty felt the hangman's hand;
But, steadfast in her life-long hope, She only saw "the promised land!
The promised land of Truth and Right The holy cause of Freedom won!
She only saw the far-off Light, And heard the People marching on!

She stood - her cheek rose-lighted still A moment, calm and iron-willed;
Then all of her which Power could kill Was mercilessly crushed and killed.
The scaffold had its radiant prey,
The Despot's minions breathed secure The proud and haughty went their way,
Spurning the dead so young and pure.
But souls like her's survive the fate Which tyrants in their might decree,
And ever live to animate
The nations struggling to be free.
Purged of the dross of earth, the fire Of one great spirit's holocaust
Will thousands wake to patriot ire Will raise to life a patriot host!

Having got that off his chest gathered up a batch of his other poems and, ignoring the possible political consequences of this project, self-published it in 1885 in a ninety page book entitled *The Beauteous Terrorist and Other Poems*. No records survive of how many copies were sold, but probably quite a few were purchased by a number of people (mainly female) who were subjects of these poems.

One of these subjects, identified only as Ragged Jane, must surely have had some apprehension at being variously described in verse as being "rough and brown, with a "Wardrobe that will not bear inspection" and with a bosom that "heaves with pure affection". But Sir Henry gallantly made up for these revelations in the final verse when he wrote:

I would not give my ragged Jane For all the peacock ladies going.
She knows the way to banish pain what she don't know is not worth knowing.

19

A Ticket in Tatts

Australians, it has been asserted, will gamble on anything, even on two flies crawling up a wall. Indeed in a sermon at Scots Church, Melbourne, in 1956, the Reverend A. Crichton Barr, awarded his fellow Australians some kind of Olympic status when he declared: "Australia has the dishonour to lead the world in gambling. Australia is the gamblers' paradise, the treasure island of the slick fellows who know there is no more gullible person than the get-rich-gambler".

The reverend gentleman was probably quite right on his last point on the gullibility of gamblers. And no one knew better how to exploit this human weakness than those two 19th Century giants of the gambling arena John Wren in Melbourne and George Adams of Tattersalls fame. Of the two, Adams proved to be the most durable since he had an uncanny knack of ducking and weaving his way around the considerable obstacles thrown in his path in various parts of the continent, whereas Wren, sticking fairly tightly to his famous, or infamous, Collingwood Tote, presented a sitting duck target to the wowsers of the day, and was thus far more vulnerable.

George Adams was born at Sandon, Herfordshire, England, in 1839 and came to Australia with his family in 1855. He was a hefty lad and found work quickly, first on a sheep station at Wellington, NSW, and then as a butcher at Goulburn and Kiama. He then quit the business of slaughtering sheep and turned to the more lucrative field of fleecing humans by acquiring the licence to the Steam Packet Inn in Kiama. He was so successful as a publican that in 1878 he was able to take over the licence of the prestigious Tattersalls Hotel in Pitt Street, acquiring the freehold to the premises in 1884 for the sum of forty thousand pounds - a fortune in those days.

Always a man of vision and imagination, he converted the Tattersalls Hotel into a Sydney showpiece by installing one of the wonders of the Pub World, the famous Marble Bar (the marble alone cost thirty two thousand pounds , and the shipping and construction considerably more). But Tattersalls was no mere pub.

It was also the headquarters of Tattersalls Club, and as such the favourite watering hole of both bookies and punters.

To help pay off his large mortgage, Adams started conducting sweepstakes on racing events and since these were fairly run they became immensely popular and soon developed into Adams' chief interest and main source of income.

The NSW Government however, threw an enormous spanner in his operations in 1892 when it enacted legislation declaring all sweeps illegal. Since Adams sold many of his sweepstakes tickets by mail to patrons all over Australia (and New Zealand) the Government turned the screws even further by placing a ban on all mail addressed to Adams or Tattersalls. Envelopes so addressed were returned to the sender.

Adams responded to this by moving his operation to Queensland which had no such legislation in the mistaken belief that he would be welcome there. However, the Queensland Government also succumbed to pressure from the anti-gambling lobby and in 1895 introduced legislation matching the NSW Act, and also imposing a ban on mail addressed to Tattersalls.

Not one to take a setback lying down, Adams quickly opened up negotiations with the Tasmanian Government which at the time was suffering severe financial difficulties and, unlike the Governments of NSW and Queensland, welcomed the opportunity to boost its revenues.

In 1896 Adams moved his entire operation to Hobart but before re-launching his sweepstakes undertook, at the invitation of the Tasmanian Government, an unusual operation to organise a lottery to sell off the assets of the Bank of Van Diemen's Land which had done a belly-flop in a big way.

This was not such a crazy idea as might seem at first glance as there was a precedent for it back in the early colonial days of New South Wales. The Bank of Australia, which had been established in Sydney in 1826, failed in 1843 having imprudently loaned too much money to reckless borrowers. They held many properties under mortgage, but times were tough and if thrown on the market would fetch far less than the amount owing on them. The name of the genius who came up with the solution to the bank's problem is not known, but it proved to be simple and effective: exploit the Australian love of gambling by raffling the unsaleable properties. In 1845 William Charles Wentworth introduced an enabling bill to this effect in the NSW Legislative Council, and the actual lottery was held in 1849. There were 11,248 prizes offered (the Bank must have had a generous loans officer!) - the first prize being the Underbank Estate of 8320 acres. The elaborately engraved tickets were printed by Harry Cooper Jarvis, and the drawing was conducted with much pomp and ceremony at the City Theatre in Market Street.

No doubt George Adams drew on the experience of the 1849 Sydney bank lottery when he carried out the similar operation in Tasmania to dispose of the assets of the Bank of Van Diemen's Land. Adams printed and sold 100 000 one pound tickets for this unusual lottery, with first prize being the Orient Hotel, Hobart, valued at thirteen thousand five hundred pounds, second prize the premises of the Bank of Van Diemen's Land in Launceston (value eight thousand pounds) and the Bank's premises in Devonport (value five thousand pounds) being third prize. There were also 3,221 minor prizes of lesser properties which the bank had acquired through careless lending practices. The lottery was an outstanding success yielding far more money for the Bank's liquidators than could have been achieved by sale of the properties on the open market. One is tempted to wonder why our modern banks didn't unload the many "dud" properties acquired through their lending frenzies of the 1980's!

Having got the bank lottery out of the way, George Adams turned his attention to his mainstream activity, the Tattersall sweeps which he re-launched from Hobart in January 1896.

These proceeded on their normal path for the next six years, yielding Tattersall profits and the Government of Tasmania much needed revenue to balance its books. A big bonus for the government was the large labour force employed by Tattersall's considerable spin-offs down the line to printers and other suppliers to the operation.

The big crunch for both Adams and the Government came in 1902 as a direct result of Federation. The new Federal Government constituted in 1901 contained a considerable number of wowsers, led by that pious old fraud King O'Malley. The group decided to make a frontal attack on gambling, with their main target being the King of the field, George Adams. The Federal Government had no power over the actual operation of lotteries and sweepstakes, as these were a matter for state legislation, but it had up its sleeve a secret weapon which the Tasmanian Government had overlooked when it supported Federation. That was in the powers vested in the newly created Postmaster General's Department. In a notice in the Commonwealth Gazette of January 31 1902, the Postmaster General announced that mail addressed to Tattersalls in Hobart would not be accepted or delivered as from March 31 1902.

This was a quite extraordinary situation, probably not matched anywhere else in the world, then or since, whereby a 'Federal government sought to suppress an organisation that operated quite legally under State law, and in fact by its operations virtually kept Tasmania afloat financially.

The Tasmanian Government was outraged by the Federal action which had been taken without any consultation with it, and decided, in consultation with Tattersalls, on various ways of circumventing the Federal ban. In effect, the Tasmanian was at war with the Federal Government!

It was then that George Adams disclosed his leadership and organising abilities. Through his wide network of agents in all parts of Australia and New Zealand he developed a series of systems circumventing the Federal postal bans. These were many and varied, the most common being the setting up of dummy addresses in and around Hobart to which agents and customers could mail their applications and money (usually postal notes) with little risk of post office detection short of postal officials actually opening suspect envelopes. Almost every Hobart Bank, and many Hobart business houses, became in effect receiving agents for Tattersalls while the number of private individuals connected with the

Tattersalls operation in some way must have extended into the hundreds over the years the bans were in operation. One of the most ingenious plans developed by Adams was one which enabled a customer to address a letter to himself (Say "John Jones") care of the No 6 Stock Exchange, Collins Street, Hobart. Prior to doing this "John Jones" supplied Tattersalls with an authority to collect the mail from the Stock Exchange.

Perhaps the majority of ticket applications received by Tattersalls each week came in bulk from his main agents scattered around the continent. These agents were not allowed to openly advertise that they were acting for Tattersalls so they used a line in their advertisements "We correspond with Hobart" which immediately alerted the punters to the true nature of the advertisement.

Getting the parcels of ticket applications (and money) to Hobart was a tricky affair because of its isolation but the agents were usually able to find parcel agents who could get the applications through. In fact some transport organisations began to specialise in this contraband parcel traffic to Tatts. There were no air services in those days, so these parcels had to be transported to Tasmania by ship, and this posed problems because not all ships had Hobart as their destination. Many went to Launceston or Davenport, and this is where the Government of Tasmania came to the party to aid Adams in a significant way.

At that time Tasmania did have a rail system which ran to the main centres, but it concentrated on passengers and bulk freight from the mines. The trains did not carry parcels, but in view of the crisis, the Government decided to make an exception in the case of Tattersalls by carrying letters and parcels from Launceston and northern ports to Hobart. To provide a fiscal base for this service the Government issued special labels (i.e. freight stamps) in denominations of ld, 3d & 6d. These were sold in bulk to

Tattersalls for use by their agents in the northern points and were affixed to parcels that had arrived by ship for onward transmission by train to Tattersalls in Hobart. This service was a closely guarded secret at the time and it was many years before the existence of these old freight stamps became known to collectors. Since most of them were destroyed by Tattersalls when the parcels were opened, they are now exceedingly scarce collector items.

The incessant war between Tattersalls and the Tasmanian Government on the one hand, and the officials of the Postmaster General's Department on the other had some bizarre side affects.

Each year Tattersalls ran a huge lottery for the Melbourne Cup, and this naturally attracted an enormous number of applications for tickets. In 1911, the Hobart branch of the Commercial Bank was acting as one of Tattersalls main receiving points. The Postmaster General's Department must have been aware of this and in the week before the Cup was run they stopped all mail to the bank seizing more than 100,000 letters, all of which had to be opened and returned to the sender, which must have been extremely costly to PMG revenue. The Bank's mail was held up for five days until the Bank gave an undertaking that they would cease to act as an agent for Tattersals.

But perhaps the oddest incident in the Tattersalls war occurred in 1924 when the Postmaster General's Department issued a new Postal Note in a denomination of five shillings and sixpence. Evidently their left hand wasn't letting their right hand know what was going on, as this was the note used almost exclusively by gamblers sending for a "Ticket in Tatts", five shillings for the ticket and sixpence for postage and result slip of the drawing. There were exceedingly red faces in the PMG's Department when the press unkindly pointed out the fact that they had issued this Postal Note to facilitate an operation they were trying to suppress. They were further embarrassed when it was pointed out that while they banned mail to Tattersalls, their staff at the Hobart GPO regularly delivered telegrams openly addressed to Tattersalls from its agents around the country placing bulk orders for tickets in Tatts

Another exquisite irony arose when the Postmaster General's Department found that they could not issue a series of Commonwealth postage stamps as had been planned for 1902 because such stamps , being interchangeable as currency between all states, would benefit Tasmania by at least eleven thousand pounds a year because of all the stamps that Tattersalls' customers used to pay for their tickets! The Commonwealth dithered on this so much that state postage stamps did not become interchangeable until 1910, and the problem forced the delay of the introduction of the first Commonwealth postage stamps until 1914.

The ban on delivery of mail to Tattersalls remained in force for 28 years until the Federal Government led by Joseph Lyons (a Tasmanian) revoked the act in 1930.

George Adams did not live to see the end of this war as he died in Hobart in 1904, aged 65, at the height of the campaign. After his death Tattersalls was formed into a company and remained in Hobart for another fifty years. In 1954 it was moved to Victoria as a result of being enticed across the Tasman Strait by John Cain's Labor Government.

During its long history, on the mainland and n Tasmania, Tattersalls; was never tainted with accusations of impropriety in its operations which is probably the reason for its success and why taking a "Ticket in Tatts" became routine for generations of Australians. But that does not mean it lacked critics. These were many and at times extremely vociferous, because to them Tatts represented a social evil. No critic was more outspoken against Tattersalls than the Reverend W. H. Judkins, a Melbourne reformer who in the latter part of the 19th Century and well into the present century saw it as his duty to campaign vigorously against what he saw as the social evils of the day. These were not only drinking and gambling (his two main targets) but barmaids, dancing, sea bathing, smoking and assorted sins of the flesh. His two main targets over many years were John Wren (under his nose in Melbourne as it were) and George Adams, further afield. When he was editor of the "Review of Reviews" in 1907 he delivered the following broadside at Tattersalls:

"Kicked out of Australia like a diseased dog is kicked out into the street, the institution known all over Australasia as Tattersalls found a welcome and a kennel in Tasmania. It was too bad to be received anywhere else, but it shivered at Tasmania's door and offered to pay for board and lodging. It was evident that its presence would spell corruption, for itself was corrupt; but what mattered that? Tasmania was unfortunate in its choice of Parliamentary representatives when the whine was made for admittance, and they sold her body and soul for what Tattersalls was willing to pay. So the bargain was made, and for sixty thousand pounds a year the evil thing was allowed to enter."

Had he been alive George Adams would not have been disturbed by this tirade, but the home grown Tasmanians would have been upset no end by Judkins' assertion that they weren't part of Australia.

But one final note on George Adams' earlier life. When he moved to Queensland in 1893, he severed his connections with that ancient institution Tattersall's Club, which is still going strong more than a century after its establishment, though it has had some rocky patches over the years. It has always been a male bastion so when it fell on hard times back in 1983, there were rumours flying around that to stay afloat it was about to lower the barriers and admit female members into the fold.

The Sydney Morning Herald sent reporter Susan Wyndham around to check the story out, but alas, it turned out to be a furphy. A committee member interviewed by the reporter said there no intention of admitting women members, and he defended the policy with the comment, "No women, no worries", To which Ms Wyndham responded in her story: "In other words, no tits for Tatts".

20

The Wentworths

It is seldom acknowledged in this day and age, but we in Australia owe and enormous debt of gratitude to the Wentworth family, particularly to William Charles Wentworth, who dominated the political and intellectual scene for much of the 19th Century. It was he who, almost single-handedly, was responsible for giving us self-government, trial by jury, freedom of the press and other benefits. He was the first to push for a constitution and for Federation and, among other achievements, helped found Sydney University. And, of course, in his younger days he, with Blaxland and Lawson, was the first to cross the Blue Mountains (1813) which led to the opening up of the continent which followed.

His great grandson William Charles ("Billy) Wentworth, also notched up a couple of remarkable achievements in his long career in and out of Parliament. He was solely responsible for getting the standardisation of the railways system off the ground. no mean feat as the rail systems had been chaotic because the states went their own way with differing gauges in the last century.

But perhaps his greatest single personal triumph was in capturing

Sydney in 1942.

He had joined the Army at the outbreak of World War II, but because of his poor eyesight was relegated to the Home Defence. As Captain in the 45th Battalion, his assignment was to guard the New South Wales coastline between Botany Bay and Stanwell Park against Japanese attack - considered a distinct possibility at the time. Captain Wentworth considered the city's defences woefully inadequate, with enormous gaps in them, but no one would heed his warnings. He got his big chance to test his theory when the Army gave him a force of seventy men and told him to carry out a mock exercise of an attack on Sydney. "Billy" Wentworth decided the only way to make the Army believe the points he had been trying to make was to make the exercise "the real thing".

And this is exactly what happened in February 1942 when Captain Wentworth's small force emerged from their bunker and went forth on what can only be described as a rampage the rest of the army would rather forget. In the following hours "Billy's" Commando group stole two buses and an Army vehicle they found unattended, created mayhem and confusion with fake calls of non-existent fires (to the Fire Brigades) and of riots (to the Police). Under the smokescreen of this confusion, they captured an Army squad sent out to investigate a fake report of a Japanese landing, then captured Battalion Headquarters in the Cronulla district (complete with an outraged and spluttering pyjama clad Colonel), "blew up" an ammunition dump, and caused untold chaos with fake messages from the HQ signals room, before "capturing" a radio station and short-circuiting the entire southern districts railway system by putting copper rods between the lines to such effect that the system was out for the next thirty-six hours. Then they went home to bed, satisfied in the knowledge that they had proved quite clearly how much damage could have resulted if a real force of Japanese had landed.

Of course all hell broke next morning as the army establishment was quite besides themselves with embarrassment, a fact they managed to conceal from the rest of the population by imposing a strict censorship blackout on the whole affair.

And what, you may well ask, did the Army Brass do when they discovered Bill's hidden strategic talents and the knowledge they had a military genius in their ranks? Did they promote him to Field Marshall and send him off to Melbourne to replace the incompetent brothel-creeper Blamey? In the immortal words of Eliza Doolittle "Not Bloody Likely." They did what any Army of any country or age would have done in the circumstances. They ignored the message and shot the messenger. They decided that Captain Wentworth's eyesight had deteriorated further, and they discharged him forthwith, thus ending a promising career!

In subsequent years, when Billy Wentworth went on to other endeavours such as Parliament it was said (frequently by his Labor Party opponents) that he was erratic or eccentric in his behaviour. And at times this appeared to be so, but then quite a few members of the large Wentworth tribe now scattered around Australia have been noted for somewhat eccentric behaviour at times.

Even the great W. C. Wentworth No 1 had his lapses. He tried to foist a Colonial Peerage on the good folks of Sydney Town but they showed much commonsense by branding this a "Bunyip Aristocracy" and laughed the idea off the map.

Then there was the time in 1840 when he launched a virtual takeover of New Zealand, an ambitious enterprise that even Alan Bond would have been hesitant about undertaking. Wentworth formed a company and had a group of Maori chiefs sign away to it 20,000 acres of land in the North Island, and a mind-boggling twenty million acres in the South Island (roughly one third of it for the sum of two hundred pounds cash in hand and a pledge by the company to pay the chiefs a further two hundred pounds a year so long as any of them lived! Wentworth was horribly upset when Governor Gipps annulled the transaction and branded the whole scheme a conspiracy.

We should not be too surprised at such lapses because the founding father of the Wentworths in Australia, Dr D'Arcy Wentworth was an eccentric of major proportions, at least until he landed on our shores. After that he calmed down a bit.

D'Arcy Wentworth's early history is remarkable in many ways, not the least because of the light it throws on the mechanics of the English class system, and of how the aristocracy went about bending the rules and the laws to protect their own interests.

D'Arcy Wentworth was born in 1764, the sixth child in a family of eight, born to D'Arcy Wentworth and his wife Martha Dickson, in Portadown, County Armagh, Ireland. The father was an Innkeeper, who could trace his ancestry back twenty generations to Robert of Wentworth Woodhouse in Yorkshire in the 13th Century. His ancestor, also a D'Arcy Wentworth went to Ireland in the 16th Century as agent in Athlone to Wentworth Dillon, fourth earl of Roscommon, and fought in the army of William III, after which he and his descendants became landowners in County Meath. However, the Wentworths had come down a lot in the world since then, though the young D'Arcy's father still claimed relationship with Lord Fitzwilliam, Earl of Stafford, one of the most powerful families in England of that time.

When young D'Arcy grew up he joined the army, serving as Ensign with the First Armagh Company of Irish Volunteers under Lord Charlemont. At that time most of the Company was fighting the insurrection of the settlers in the American War of Independence, but D'Arcy was not required to leave Ireland. While in the Army service he served an apprenticeship in medicine with intent of securing a posting in the East India Company.

After leaving the army he went to London to further his medical experience in the Hospitals there and to meet up with his distant relative, Lord Fitzwilliam, hoping he would assist in getting the coveted East India Company posting. Initially Lord Fitzwilliam refused to acknowledge kinship with this blow-in from Ireland. But D'Arcy was persistent and appears to have had a winning way as contemporaries from this period described him as tall, burly and handsome with blue eyes, and eventually Lord Fitzwilliam relented and acknowledged kinship, and introduced the young Irishman into London society. It was a decision Lord Fitzwilliam had much cause for regret considering the enormous trouble the young man brought down on the family in the next few years.

The position with the East India Company never did come through, and young D'Arcy Wentworth was living it up in London, far beyond his means. He decided to solve his financial problems in an unusual way for a doctor, by becoming a highwayman in his spare time. Which might have been alright if he had been competent at the game, but he wasn't.

In the next two years (1787-1789) he was arrested on charges of highway robbery four times - and on each occasion he faced the gallows since this was a capital offence. And each time, by one means or another, the Fitzwilliam family managed to bail him out. They could have had little sympathy for this exceedingly troublesome young man who had appeared out of the blue to disrupt their lives, but there were considerations well beyond saving D'Arcy's skin (or neck) involved here. Had they let him go to the gallows, or even been convicted, the event would have resulted in enormous publicity reflecting on such a powerful family. In coming to the rescue of D'Arcy they were serving their own interests as well as his. So they saw to it that at each of his trials he had the very best legal talent to get him off the hook. And that clearly meant the ends justifying any means.

The first occasion was no great problem. D'Arcy had agreed to go to Botany Bay as surgeon on the Charlotte in the First Fleet which sailed on May 1787, and he was discharged without a conviction being recorded. But the Judge's faith in D'Arcy's promise to turn up at the docks at First Fleet sailing time was sadly misplaced. He reneged on the deal, went AWL and the Fleet sailed off into the blue without him.

But his narrow escape from the gallows surely must have given him a huge fright. Most individuals would have been shocked to the core by the experience. But D'Arcy must have been either stupid, or very desperate for money, because he kept on his criminal ways, and of course, was caught again, and again.

The next time the family lawyers got him off with a plea of "it was clearly a case of mistaken identity, Your Honour". And because the accused was a relative of Lord Fitzwilliam, the judge discharged him. The next time wasn't so easy as there were several witnesses. But when the case came to trial, Lo, a miracle had occurred, and the witnesses all had serious lapses of memory, were very hazy in their recollections, or couldn't recall who was up who at the time. It is amazing how bouts of amnesia can occur after the distribution of a few sovereigns in the right places. There may be more innocent explanations of what occurred, but it is difficult to think what they might be.

By this time the Fitzwilliam family must have been browned off with this Irish relative who was causing them so much angst. And the London rozzers must have been distressed by the way this young hoon kept slipping through their fingers. Possibly they set a trap, because on the final occasion he fell into their charge it was because he was caught red-handed in his highway-activities. They had him cold and this time no smart-arse lawyer could get him off. So they thought.

It would have been wonderful to have been a fly on the wall in the family estate drawing room as the Fitzwilliams and their lawyers deliberated on how they could get young D'Arcy (and themselves) off the hook. In the end they resorted to the original plan after he had been arrested the first time, namely to ship him off to Botany Bay. But this time they obviously took steps to ensure that he wouldn't backslide again. We can only guess at what these measures involved, but they worked.

When D'Arcy Wentworth fronted up to the Old Bailey in the Sessions which began on December 9 1789, Counsel immediately arose and addressed the court thus: "My Lord, Mr Wentworth, the prisoner at the bar, has taken passage to go in a fleet to Botany Bay, and has obtained an appointment in it as assistant surgeon, and desires to be discharged immediately".

The strange thing about this statement is that it was not made by the Counsel for the defence, but by the Prosecuting Counsel. They say that a nod is as good as a wink to a blind horse but even the blindest of Blind Freddies, would have recognised that somewhere behind the scenes a deal had been struck. His Honour certainly was under no misapprehension, as he immediately discharged the prisoner into the charge of the master of the Neptune, about to sail for Botany Bay with the Second Fleet.

Thus was justice administered in Merrie old England in the bad old days, confirming the fact that there was, and probably always will be, one set of laws for the rich and famous, and another for the rest of us. Which thought could have been little consolation for the thousands of men and women then incarcerated in the prison hulks awaiting their turn to be shipped off to the new world for such petty crimes as stealing a loaf of bread or poaching a rabbit.

But in a funny way, this travesty of justice, where a person could escape the hangman's noose four times simply because of his family connections, did make sense of a sort. A powerful, and well respected family escaped having its name dragged through the mud by the gutter press of the day. They got the culprit out of their hair for ever, and for their country's good; and his talents as a surgeon, which were in extremely short supply at the time, could at least be put to good use on the ship and in the far off colony of New South Wales were there was such great need of them.

And that is how D'Arcy Wentworth, surgeon, came to arrive at Port Jackson in 1790 on the Neptune, the "Hell Ship" of the Second Fleet on which almost a quarter of the convicts died of disease and malnutrition.

It cannot have been a pleasant experience for D'Arcy Wentworth, and perhaps the horrors of the voyage, and the knowledge that he could never return to his native land, had at last made such an impression, that he decided to put the ugly past behind him and make a fresh start in this new land. And that is exactly what he did. In the subsequent years he does not seem to have put a foot wrong, and in turn held such positions as Superintendent of Convicts on Norfolk Island, Assistant Surgeon and eventually Principal Surgeon of Sydney Town, A Justice of the Peace, Magistrate and then Chief Magistrate, Superintendent of Governor Macquarie's Reformed Police Force, Treasurer of the Police Fund, Personal Physician to Governor Macquarie, one of the Commissioners of the Parramatta Turnpike Road and one of the founding Directors of the Bank of New South Wales, the colony's first bank.

Along the way he received from various governors as rewards for his public services a number of land grants totalling more than 17,000 acres, including one grant made "for his diligence in pursuing and stamping out the activities of highwaymen in the colony". In the process he accumulated such wealth that on his death in 1827, aged 63, he was adjudged to be the wealthiest man in the colony. Not a bad achievement for someone who had four times stood in the dock of Old Bailey charged with highway robbery! And it is perhaps appropriate that on his gravestone there should be engraved the message: *In my father's house there are many mansions.*

Stories like this were not uncommon in the hurly burly years of the convict period, and Dr D'Arcy Wentworth's rise and rise in the colony might have passed into the footnotes of history but for the fact that throughout his life he was just as active in the bedroom as he had been on the highways of England. Arising from that came the foundation of the remarkable Wentworth dynasty that was to have such an impact on various aspects of Australian history.

On the way out to Port Jackson in the Neptune, the good doctor took up with a convict girl Catherine Crowley, and by her had three sons, the first born of these being the remarkable William Charles Wentworth.

When Catherine Crowley died in 1800, D'Arcy immediately formed a liaison with another convict girl Ann Lawes and they produced another seven children. Of course he didn't marry either girl. In those days gentleman of breeding didn't go that far. But, to his credit, D'Arcy Wentworth acknowledged all ten little Wentworth bastards and provided for their education and upbringing, and in his will provided for their various needs, which is a lot more than some modern parents do for their legitimate broods.

All in all, seeing the benefits that ultimately flowed to Australia, as a result of D'Arcy being exiled rather than hanged, perhaps we should not judge Lord Fitzwilliam too harshly for bending the law as he so obviously did back in 1789.

21

The Tall Poppies

Visitors to these shores have often commented on the way that Australians seem to delight in cutting down to size the so-called Tall Poppies in their midst. What they tend to overlook is that this is a very selective process carefully honed to almost ritualistic forms over two centuries.

The Tall Poppy syndrome goes back to the earliest days of white settlement, though it was known by other names in those times. It was all part of the grim determination of the Emancipists (the ex-convicts) and the Free Settlers, particularly the Irish, to cast off the shackles of the British class system which had ground them down so much over the centuries. Australia was supposed to be the New Land, the classless Utopian society of the free, which meant the freedom to thumb their noses at the "Toffs" in their midst. This was expressed beautifully by Francis Adams in his comment: "This is a true republic, the truest, as I take it, in the world. In England the average man feels that he is inferior, in America that he is superior; in Australia he feels that he is equal".

Adams' comment about the difference with America is quite

significant. Here were two ex-British colonies, one of which had completely thrown off the ties with Britain, the other still trying to do so. Yet they went down separate paths, probably because America never did become a dumping ground for thousands of convicts as had Australia. The oppression experienced by the convicts in the first half century of white settlement had no parallel in America, and it brought in its train fierce anti-authoritarian attitudes expressed in the old piece of bush doggerel:

The Master Class can kiss my arse. I've got a Guv'mint job at last.

Frank Thompson, an American who has been associated with Australian publishing over many years, summed it all up neatly when he noted the differences between our two countries: "It has always seemed to me that the real differences between Australians and Americans was in how each defined the word 'Freedom' To most Americans I think the word means liberty, the right to believe, the right to do within the law what one wants to do. For Australians I suspect the word freedom means equality. There is something in the Australian psyche that profoundly dislikes some smart-arse up there parading his brain. Socially, it is one step above flashing, and not all that dissimilar. It is perhaps part of the Tall Poppy Syndrome that compels us to make sure that no bugger thinks he is any better than anyone else."

Although not originally an Australian term, Tall Poppy gained wide acceptance in the early 1930's when the crusading Labor Premier of New South Wales , Jack Lang, used it frequently in his election campaigns when he proposed a policy of high taxation of the wealthier classes whom he referred to as the Tall Poppies In his book, *The Turbulent Years*, published in 1970, he explained that what he had meant when he used the term back in 1930 was anyone earning more than ten pounds a week!.

Some years further down the track (in 1973) another prominent

Labor politician, Clyde Cameron, as Minister for Labor and National Service in the Whitlam Government, waged war on the Public Service Board for awarding huge salary increases to what he described as the "Fat Cats" of the Public Service, a term that immediately gained wide currency.

Not everyone agreed with the idea that Tall Poppies and Fat Cats should be laid low and in 1975 a former Liberal Prime Minister, John Grey Gorton, rushed to their rescue with the comment: "Labor is obsessed with the Tall Poppies, and seems determined to pull them down. But Tall Poppies, more and more are what this country needs. The chance to grow to a height is the chance for many to express themselves."

The point that John Gorton, and many overseas commentators on the subject, miss is that Australians as a whole are not obsessed with chopping down the Tall Poppies (or Fat Cats) per se. They are now, and always have been highly selective in the pruning process.

The Tall Poppies selected for lopping, tend to be the those who "bung it on a bit", or who (in old terms) are caught "putting on the jam" or "putting on the side", or who are a "bit above themselves". In other words considered to be phoney by fellow Australians, making themselves sitting-duck targets for the Tall Poppy hunters.

On the other hand, there are heaps of Tall Poppies, quite decent blokes (and even a few Blokesses) who don't make a fuss of their wealth or power and are left alone, even though they may have a Rolls or a Merc or two stacked away out the back.

It must be admitted that a somewhat different measure is sometimes applied to visiting Tall Poppies, particularly those from England than is the case with the local breed. Tall Poppies from the other side of the world carry a bit of lead in their saddlebags so far as the locals are concerned and often come unstuck as a result of not being able to properly gauge the egalitarian temperature Down Under. A couple of well reported instances illustrate the problems experienced by the visiting Fat Cat.

Back in 1981 the well known English TV Presenter, Michael Parkinson, was visiting our shores and unhappily attended a charity luncheon where all the waitressing was undertaken by volunteer society ladies, a situation that Parky would not have experienced in the more class conscious Old Dart. When Parky was served white wine instead of the red that he had ordered, he became a trifle terse with the help. The offended matron proved to be a dab hand in the matter of cutting down Tall Poppies as she directed a well deserved missile in Parky's direction: "We have come a long way from the Yorkshire pits, haven't we?", she snapped.

The other example concerns an even taller Tall Poppy - Sir Larry Lamb, former editor of the London "Sun", who was brought to Australia by Rupert Murdoch to do a stint as Editor of "The Australian". On his arrival on these shores Sir Larry was somewhat dismayed with the amenities (or lack of them) in the offices assigned to him. Not at all what he was used to in the press palaces of Fleet Street. He decided to rectify the situation and ordered a private bathroom to be built next to his office. When this move was relayed to Rupert Murdoch, he immediately countermanded the instructions and told his management man to relay a message to Sir Larry: "Tell Larry he's in Australia now. If he wants a piss he can do it out the window".

Which only goes to show that when it comes to the crunch the Tall Poppies are not above cutting down to size other Tall Poppies of the realm. Needless to say, in the example quoted above, Sir Larry's departure back to London soon followed.

The much criticised Tall Poppy Syndrome should be seen for what it really is. A kind of selective egalitarianism.

And what's so wrong with that?

22

Australia's My Lei

The people of many countries should carry a burden of guilt from misdeeds of compatriots in former times upheaval since guilt is, or should be, a collective memory of a nation's conscience. Yet many people go to extremes to deny such a thing as collective guilt.

The Japanese are still strenuously denying their collective crimes of World War II such as the ghastly germ warfare experiments carried out in its factories in Manchuria, its official role in conscripting tens of thousands of "comfort women" for the use and abuse of its soldiers, and even such well documented atrocities as the Sandakan march. Over on the other side of the world, its wartime ally Germany is still writhing in a morass of guilt over the Holocaust, while its next door neighbour and ex-enemy France is still desperately trying to cover up the role of its top level citizen collaborators who assisted the Gestapo in the round-up of "undesirables" to be fed into the gas chambers of Belsen and other destinations of horror.

So deep are the open and ugly wounds of these events they can even reach out to the far side of the globe to Australia, as witness the ferocious and ugly eruption of emotion which followed the 1995 Miles Franklin Literary award to Helen Demidenko/Darville's novel, *The Hand That Signed the Paper*.

It seems many people on all sides of the political or racial fence are quite unprepared, or unwilling , to face the fact that in times of crisis perfectly ordinary men and women can be turned into monsters, ready and willing to commit the most monstrous crimes in the service of their state. If we accept the premise that this might be so, should it not be time for all Australians to be doing a little soul -searching to some of the dark events of the country's murky past - the many deliberate acts of genocide and ethnic cleansing carried out since 1788 by white settlers against the aborigines?

Unfortunately, to even raise this question is akin to being accused of heresy and blasphemy. Inevitably when such questions are raised the instant disclaimers of guilt on the grounds that all this was totally beyond their control; that it happened a long, long time ago when standards and conditions were different.

It is true that many of these events did happen in the far distant past, but how about a date like 1926? Is that far distant in our history? It is certainly within my lifespan and within the lifetimes of substantial numbers of my fellow citizens. Yet 1926 was the year of the last (known) massacre of tribal aborigines by an official Police Punitive Expedition sent out for that express purpose. It occurred in the Kimberleys of Western Australia and is well documented in the records of WA Police archives and clearly set out in the documentation of the Wood Royal Commission which enquired into affair. Yet as late as 1994 a Perth newspaper devoted a considerable amount of space to an article attempting to deny that such a massacre occurred, despite all the evidence when it learned that the first ever book on the event *The Forrest River Massacres*, by Neville Green was about to be published by the

Fremantle Arts Centre Press —a case of a desperate cover up in advance of an event!

It is not surprising that Western Australia should have been able to claim the dishonour of such official acts of violence against the aborigines long after other states of the Commonwealth had relinquished such policies. From its very beginning, the West went its own way and built up an appalling reputation in its treatment of the native population both by officialdom and the settlers in acts and attitudes. The latter have by no means been extinguished with the passing of the years.

The pattern of violence towards the aborigines was a consistent one extending over more than a century and for half that period one family of missionaries, the Gribbles, fought a valiant but largely unsuccessful campaign to expose the excesses and have them rectified.

After a successful missionary career in the Eastern states, the Reverend J. B. Gribble was brought to Western Australia by the Church of England Missionary Society in 1885 to establish a mission station on the Gascoyne River, but the mission was poorly planned and staffed and so strongly opposed by the settlers that it had to be abandoned.

Somewhat embittered by the experience, and shocked by the treatment of aborigines in the district, the Reverend Gribble in 1886 gave an interview with a Melbourne newspaper condemning in strong language the "assignment system" in force in Western Australia. Under this system bush aborigines, both men and women, were hunted down by parties of settlers and taken, chained by the neck, to the nearest station. There they were handed a paper (which they could not read) told to make a "X. as a signature and thus were legally assigned, virtually as a slave, to the station owner. If they absconded they were hunted down by police and taken to

Perth, where they were sentenced (usually for a six months period) to detention on Rottnest Island, then a penal outpost. For the duration of their detention they were taken out of cells each day and two by two chained by the neck to the nearest gumtree. After this they were taken back to their assigned property.

On the stations they were flogged at will by the settlers for any misdemeanour. The women were simply treated as sex objects by the settlers and station hands. If any offspring resulted from these forced couplings they were unceremoniously disposed of immediately after birth. One of the most telling points in the Rev Gribble's statement was that on the northern stations there were no half castes. The station owners saw to that with their policy of instant infanticide.

The article caused quite a stir at the time but no action in the way of reform followed, so the disillusioned missionary returned to the east and established the successful Yarrabah Mission in North Queensland.

In 1896 the Western Australian Missionary society made another attempt to conquer the north, this time at Forrest River, near the mouth of the Cambridge Gulf in the Kimberleys. Although this was a better equipped and manned mission, led by Rev Harold Hale and a party of four other missionaries, it also failed, largely due to fierce opposition from local aborigines. The embryo mission was abandoned.

In 1913 the newly appointed Bishop of the North West districts, Bishop Trower, personally took charge of an attempt to re-establish the old Forrest Mission on the 1896 site. So many problems were encountered, that the Bishop sent an urgent appeal out to the Reverend Ernest Gribble, son of the Rev J. B. Gribble. As a schoolboy he had been with his father on the Gascoyne mission attempt of 1885.

At that time he was the Rector of Christ Church, Gosford, NSW, and had just received an offer from the Queensland Government of the position of Protector of Aborigines in North Queensland. He decided to reject this offer and accept the offer of Bishop Trower to take charge of the infant and struggling Forrest River Mission, which also carried with it the post of Protector of Aborigines for the Northern Districts of the Kimberleys. No doubt in the years to come he would have much cause to regret the new career path he had chosen, a path that destroyed his vocation and his health.

At that time the tiny town of Wyndham, some fifty miles up the Cambridge Gulf from the Forrest River Mission, was the only major settlement in the northern sector of the Kimberleys and the mission was reliant on it to a certain extent as an outlet for the meagre quantities of vegetables grown on the mission and as a shipping point for the cattle produced on the 100,000 acre "run" of the Mission - the Wyndham killing works had not then been established. They were built during World War I.

Once the Mission was established some 200 aborigines drifted in and out of the Mission on a more or less regular basis, and came to be regarded as Mission Blacks. Perhaps another thousand scattered in isolated pockets throughout the north had some irregular contact, or were known by name and tribe to the Missionaries.

But it was a wild frontier country, then and to some extent still is. Back in 1968 a Sydney writer named Athol Thomas described in *The Bulletin* a recent visit he had made to Wyndham. When he wandered into the Port Hotel, he engaged in conversation with a local waterside worker who was dressed in the current style of grubby shorts, boots without socks and a black singlet. The conversation opened briskly: "So you are up here to write about us", said the wharfie, "Put this in, mate. Cambridge Gulf is the arsehole of the world and Wyndham is 65 miles up it".

Wyndham was a "white town" and relations between the whites in the town and district and the district aborigines had long been discordant, and occasionally violent, usually over two different issues, cattle and women.

The aborigines, without any traditional system of ownership, were wont to spear a bullock when they were unable to find food and this invariably led to trouble between the spearer's tribe and the owner of the beast. But trouble over aboriginal women had long been a running sore throughout the Kimberleys because of the scarcity of white women in the pioneering period, and the appalling attitudes of the white station owners towards the black women who they considered were there for the use of themselves and their men at will. There were numerous reports in the 1920's of station owners taking possession of the young wives of their black stockmen and chaining them up to the bed posts until they "got the message" and agreed to submit to the sexual demands of the Bossman. Such owners quickly earned the reputation of "Gin-men" and the office of the Protector of Aborigines was often forced to withdraw assigned black labour from such properties until the owner or manager promised to turn over a new leaf.

It was one of these incidents that sparked the Forrest River massacres of 1926. The culprit was Frederick Hay, a notorious 'gin-man' of the district whose property Nulla Nulla station was at the time under just such assignment ban.

Hay was a returned soldier who had worked at various labouring jobs in the Wyndham area after World War I. In 1921 he teamed up with another returned soldier named Leopold Overheu to lease the Nulla Nulla station of 320,000 hectares when it was opened up under a Soldier Settlement scheme. It was a marginal operation not returning enough income to support them both, so Overheu did the books and worked full time at the Wyndham meatworks, while Hay ran the station with the help of a station hand named James Dunnett - another notorious 'gin-man'.

As early as 1922, Hay was the subject of complaints over his treatment of aboriginal women and violence towards his black station workers. He had a savage dog which he trained to attack aborigines - until one of latter managed to spear it. In 1924 Hay seriously injured one of his station aborigines by striking him over the head with a rifle butt, but no charges were laid. It was almost unheard of for any white man to be charged with assault of a native. In the same year he took an aboriginal woman named Angelina from her husband, Barnabus, and shared her with James Dunnett. It was as a result of this, that his black labour force was withdrawn. Incidentally, when I refer here to the taking of wives by force, we are not referring to adult women. Aboriginal girls at that time had a rough time of it, whether in black or white camps, as at puberty they were assigned to a member of their tribe, usually an elder, and that was that. The "wives" that the likes of Hay, commandeered for their sexual pleasures were girls as young as twelve.

Things came to a head on Nulla Nulla in May 1926, when Hay was again on the "black list" for assigned labour. Whilst out on patrol of his property he met up with one of his ex-workers named Lumbia, a man in his forties, who was accompanied by his child-wife Anulgoo, and by Goolool, the young wife of Gumbol. The story that then unfolded, as told by Lumbia in his confession and corroborated by both girls is a horrifying one, but probably not unusual for the time and place.

At the approach of Hay, Lumbia had in the usual tradition laid his spears on the ground to signify that his intentions were peaceful. Hay dismounted from his horse, then indicated to the small party that he intended to have sex with Anulgoo, there and then. He took the precaution of breaking Lumbia's spears in two, undressed and proceeded to rape Anulgoo while the others stood off watching. Having completed his act, Hay then told Lumbia that he was taking Anulgoo back to the homestead. This was too much for Lumbia who, when Hay turned his back, dashed forward and seized the business half of one of his broken spears and plunged it in Hay's back, killing him instantly. The three aborigines then fled the scene hastily, well aware what retribution would follow.

Hay's naked and blackened body, partly consumed by scavengers was found three days later by a search party led by Constable St. Jack of Wyndham. The blacktracker in the party reported that there were only three footprints leading from the scene of the crime, one of an adult male and two by small females. Constable St Jack, a rookie to the district, failed to understand the significance of this, and paid much more credence to the fact that some distance off there were tracks showing a group of aborigines had passed by some days earlier. His report on his gruesome find was totally distorted, probably more by ignorance than intent, to the effect that Hay had been murdered by a tribe of aborigines.

There was immediate outrage in the (white) community that one of their own should have been murdered by blacks. It was usually the other way around. They demanded of the police that something be done, and be done, urgently to bring the culprits to book.

At that time the Wynham police force comprised only three men. Sergeant Arthur Harold Buckland, who was in charge, but in poor health and nearing retirement, Constable St Jack, a recent arrival, and Constable Dennis Hastings Regan, an experienced officer, who was attached to Wyndham but was posted at nearby Turkey Creek Police Station.

Although there was the clearest evidence by the blacktracker that there was only one culprit to the crime, the police mounted a massive expedition to track down what they (mistakenly) believed to be a whole tribe of culprits. From the size of the of the team, it was clear that this was to be a Punitive Expedition with a "take no prisoners" objective. And such an Expedition would have had the almost unanimous support and approval of the white population of the district - the exception being the Rev Gribble.

The expedition members were:

- Constable Regan, (Leader),
- Constable St Jack,
- Special Constable Bernard Patrick O'Leary (A pastoralist of Galway Station),
- Special Constable Richard John Jolly, unemployed wharf-laborer and former meat works hand,
- Leonard Rupert Overheu, Hay's partner and part-lessee of Nulla Nulla station,
- Daniel Murname, a veterinary surgeon from Victoria, who happened to be carrying out an assignment in the Kimberleys,
- Jim McDonald, alias Mulga Jim, a police tracker,
- Frank. a police tracker from Turkey Creek police station,
- Jacob, a tracker from Wyndham police station,
- Charlie, an aborigine employed by O'Leary,
- Windie, an aboriginal added as a special tracker,
- Sulieman, an Afghan/aborigine, added as a special tracker,
- Tommy, alias Doort, employed by Overheu,
- Goolara, alias Lyddie, Tommy's wife.

All members. except Goolara. were armed with .44 Winchester rifles or shotguns with a supply of more than 400 rounds of side arms, mostly six shot revolvers. Each member of party was mounted and the expedition comprised 32 animals, including mules and packhorses.

This formidable mini army was split into two groups, one led by Constable St. Jack and one led by Constable Regan. They set out in different directions but met up as a combined group several days later. The patrol left Wyndham on June 1 1926, and was out in the bush for three weeks, during which period an unknown number of aborigines were shot.

While the expedition was away on this initial foray, the Reverend Gribble became deeply disturbed being concerned for his mission charges and heedful of his duties as Protector of Aborigines. He was well aware that the Expedition was a punitive one, quite likely to shoot any blacks they sighted. Through his network of contacts with the aborigines on the mission and registered with it, he was quickly able to ascertain how Hay died and Lumbia's name as the culprit. He also knew Lumbia's present whereabouts.

While it very much went against his grain to turn natives in , he had done so in the past where serious crimes had been committed, and he decided to do so again in this case to save a number of innocent victims being shot. So he officially informed Sergeant Buckland that Lumbia was the sole perpetrator and where he was to be found.

When the expedition returned in the third week of June Buckland sent them out again to apprehend Lumbia. This they achieved without incident on June 26, but they continued on patrol until July 4, when a further slaughter of aborigines occurred at Dala.

With Lumbia in custody, having confessed to the crime and been charged with murder, the district quietened down a bit, but members of the two expeditions freely talked with friends and soon rumours of what had taken place were flying around thick and fast. In this period Overheu told a fellow worker at the meatworks that it had been "like war out there".

Meanwhile out at the Forrest River Mission, the Rev Gribble was making his own investigations and what he found disturbed him deeply. Some thirty members of his flock had simply gone missing. Vanished from the face of the earth. His worst fears were confirmed when a member of the Police Expedition, Tommy, who was employed by Overheu, troubled by his conscience, went to Gribble and, according to the minister, pulled the plug on what had happened in the period of almost five weeks they had been out on patrol. According to Tommy, the white members of the expedition had shot every aborigine they encountered, men, women and children, and then had carefully burnt the bodies and scattered the charred bones far and wide.

Tommy gave specific details of sites of the killings so Gribble went out with a team of trusted mission members who knew the country intimately. At the sites nominated by Tommy they came on much evidence of fires and brought back with them quantities of burnt bone fragments.

But Gribble's enquiries could not be kept secret in such a small community, and they virtually sealed Tommy's death warrant. Tommy simply disappeared. His body was never found, but the native "grapevine" claimed that he had been shot by his employer Overheu. This could never be proved and no one was charged over the loss of the only important eyewitness to the massacres.

Meanwhile disturbing reports of the massacres had reached district police headquarters in Broome and the officer in charge, Police Inspector Douglas went to Wyndham to investigate. Douglas immediately ran up against a wall of silence and open hostility from the civilian population, and obstruction and evasions by local police. He had no back-up staff to help him with his enquiries but came to the conclusion, that a number aborigines, possibly as many as thirty, had been killed, but he had not been able to establish where, when or by whom. He concluded that there was ample circumstantial evidence to justify a full police enquiry.

His findings in a sixteen page report was sent off to the Commissioner of Police in Perth. The Commissioner's office passed a summary on to the Government, but no further action was taken. Back at the Forrest River Mission, the Reverend Gribble was becoming increasingly frustrated. He had reported all the facts to his Mission Headquarters and the Headquarters of the Protectorate of Aborigines without arousing any apparent interest In typical Gribble style he decided to "blow the whistle" as his father had done 40 years earlier in similar circumstances by going public — i.e. spilling the beans to the press.

The Perth *Daily News* broke the story on September 2 with a claim that seven natives had been shot and burned on the Marndoc Reserve. The following morning the more conservative *West Australian* newspaper joined in with a statement by the Minister for the Aborigines Department, J W Hickey, saying that while effecting the arrest of Hay's killer, seven other aborigines had been shot by blacktrackers another month passed before the public became aware that Europeans were implicated in killings. The Government was ducking for cover on every level at this point. *The Sunday Truth*, on October 23, ran a banner headline: "ALARMING REPORT THAT NATIVES WERE HORRIBLY MURDERED IN THE NORTH IS MET BY A CONSPIRACY OF SILENCE."

Actually it was the sensational treatment being given to the story in the press of the eastern states which eventually forced the Government's hand. The Perth press had continued to play down the story from day one. In December the Government caved in and announced the appointment of a Royal Commission to be headed by Senior Stipendiary Magistrate George Tuttle Wood who would conduct the enquiry for a stipend of three guineas a day, or two guineas while travelling to and from the Kimberleys by ship. These fees will raise the eyebrows of our present day silks used to commanding up to $4000 a day, plus expenses, for their services. The Commissioner was to be assisted by Inspector Douglas.

It has long been held in political circles that no Royal Commission should be set up if the Government is not reasonably certain what the results will be. In most cases this means appointing a Commissioner whose views are well known in advance to be along the lines of official thinking.

There is no reason to suspect that the Kimberley Massacres Royal Commission was influenced in this way as Commissioner Wood clearly sought to get to the bottom of the killings. But his was almost a hopeless task from the start given the continued obstructions and outright lying he encountered from the Wyndham police, the openly hostile attitudes of most of the Wyndham community and the disappearance or unavailability of key Aboriginal witnesses and of course , the loss of the key witness Tommy.

His eventual report, presented on May 21 1927, ran to more than a hundred foolscap pages, mainly of tiny six point type in double columns to the page, makes depressing reading. That an unknown number of aborigines had been killed and their bodies burned was beyond doubt given the mass of evidence presented. But identifying the victims was almost as difficult as deciding when and where each expired, let alone who fired the fatal shot in each case. The witnesses, police and civilian alike, were united in their determination to draw a curtain of silence over the whole affair. They saw nothing and heard nothing in the whole five weeks the patrols were out. They lied their heads off and Commissioner Wood was quite blunt in saying so in his report.

In the prelude to the evidence his frustration at times became evident. He pointed out that while the implicated parties (white) were represented by well paid advocates, the Forrest River Mission and the Aboroigines and the aboriginal trackers were not represented and thus were at a serious disadvantage throughout. He complained strongly that Sulieman, Windie and Frank, three important (coloured) witnesses were absent because local police who had held them in custody until three days before the enquiry began had allowed them to escape and "couldn't find them" during all the time the Commission sat. Wood was scathing on this issue: "I must record my displeasure that those trackers were not produced before the Commission, and I cannot exonerate the Police at Wyndham from responsibility for their absence or for the very slight effort that seems to have been made, when their absence was discovered, to secure their return and attendance".

Commissioner Wood dealt in considerable detail with the inconsistencies, evasions and lying of the white witnesses including Daniel Murname, the visiting veterinarian, the only "outsider" who, unless he was personally guilty , might have been expected to break ranks. Not so. He stuck with the team and Wood, with apparent exasperation noted: " Inspector Douglas disbelieved the statements of the whites and I agree with him. Hence, I have no hesitation in bracketing Murname with the rest of the whites who did not scruple to lie to the Commission".

Commissioner Wood found that a number of aborigines had died while in the custody of either Constable St John or Constable Regan, and that the constables were responsible for these deaths. What happened then? Constable St Jack and Constable Regan were charged with murder but magistrate Kidson discharged them on grounds of lack of evidence. No disciplinary charges were ever brought against them, despite the flagrant breaches revealed in the Commission evidence. Both were immediately restored to the force and all back pay made up, and both were posted to new positions outside the Kimberleys. Regan later resigned from the force but St John remained in the force, rose to the rank of sergeant and retired at the age of 60. Sgt Buckland, who had been in charge at Wyndham was transferred to Roebourne. No charge was ever brought against any of the white civilians on the expedition.

All members of the expedition maintained a tight lip in subsequent years, refusing to give interviews and all went to their graves without making any admissions of guilt.

Lumbia had been tried for the murder of Hay before the Royal Commission commenced. Not understanding what was going on he made a dash from the court, but was quickly recaptured and chained to a post outside the court while proceedings continued inside. He did not have any legal representation, and was quickly found guilty and sentenced to death, but this was commuted to life after appeals by the Australian Board of Missions.

The Reverend Gribble was the biggest loser of all from the events of 1926. Not only had his whistle blowing been in vain, since no culprit was brought to justice for the massacres, but his health was shattered and there was open hostility towards him throughout the white community of the district. His position became untenable. His employer, the Australian Board of Missions, were well aware of the problem but hesitated to take any action against him for fear of making him a martyr. Frankly they considered him a troublemaker and an embarrassment to the Board, but in the Eastern States he had been elevated to the status of hero so they were content to bide their time.

Their opportunity came later in 1927 when Professor A. P. Elkin visited the Kimberleys on a research mission. He took an intense dislike to Gribble and filed a secret report to the Australian Board of Missions commenting adversely on Gribble and the run down state of the Forrest River Mission. On September 1 1927 the Reverend Gribble received his official notification that he had been dismissed from his command of the Mission. The same mail that brought the dismissal notice also brought news of his mother's death.

He was then in his 60th year and could easily have retired, but he felt his work with the aborigines must continue and volunteered to be chaplain of Palm Island, a settlement in Northern Queensland. There he remained for 29 years. In that period he wrote two books dealing with his years as a missionary, *Forty Years With the Aborigines* (published 1930) and *A Despised Race* (published 1933). The first book made only a single paragraph reference to the Kimberley massacres. Obviously the whole affair had been so traumatic that he could never put pen to paper to give his version of events. A few months before he retired he was awarded the Order of the British Empire.

He died in1957, aged 89. He had started out in life as a young man determined to follow in the substantial footsteps of his father in the missionary field. But he was always, like his father, to serve on the outer frontiers where life was raw, violent and full of racist prejudices, which can perhaps be best summed up in two editorial quotes from *The Northern Territory Times* of Darwin from that far-off period: "The only things that have hitherto proved of any value in bringing the niggers to their senses have been dogs and revolvers" (1875) and "It is quite clear that the aboriginal question can only be settled to the satisfaction of the white man by a liberal use of powder and Shot" (1891).

There are uncanny parallels between what happened in the

Kimberleys in 1926 and the My Lei massacre in Vietnam in 1968 when Lieutenant William Calley led a small force from "C" for Charley Company of the American Division 15/11th Infantry Brigade into the small hamlet of My Lei believed (incorrectly) to be sheltering Vietcong forces. In a rampage that lasted more than four hours the men killed more than a hundred people, elderly men, women and children, repeatedly raped and sodomised many of the women before killing them, destroying the village in the process.

Just consider for a moment the following similarities between the Kimberley and My Lei massacres:

1. Both operations were officially sanctioned, the Kimberley one by the Sergeant in charge at Wyndham and the My Lei one by divisional headquarters.
2. Both were organised as "Payback" operations, in the Kimberleys for the killing of a white man, in Vietnam because US forces had sustained heavy casualties in that general area.
3. Both operations had strong racial overtones. In the Kimberleys it was to teach the blacks a lesson once and for all; in Vietnam just to "Kill the Gooks".
4. The white attackers were heavily armed in both operations. The victims were either poorly armed or (in the case of women, old men and children) totally without defences.
5. Both operations were mounted on faulty intelligence information
6. In the My Lai operation not a single shot was fired against the US troops in the whole four hour exercise. In the Kimberleys the expedition members did not report any attack on them at any time in the five week

long operation.

7. In both operations there was no known "body count". Initial reports at My Lei gave a figure of thirty, this was later extended to 109 but this appears a conservative figure. In the Kimberleys the probable death toll was around thirty.
8. News of the massacres was known to a large number of people soon after the forces involved returned to base.
9. In both instances there was an immediate attempt at a "cover up " by senior forces and this was continued long after the event In the Kimberleys case Police Headquarters in Perth took no action on Inspector Douglas' quite damning report. In the My Lai case the Pentagon instructed Major John Powell (later General Powell, Chief of Staff of US Armed forces) to investigate rumours of a massacre at My Lai. Major Powell reported back that accounts of any such massacre were malicious fiction. In the Kimberleys only one man was responsible for the killing of the white man Hay, and the Police ignored clear evidence it was so. In Vietnam the intelligence that My Lai villagers were hiding Vietcong was patently false and could have been established within minutes of the operation starting.
10. The news of the massacres at both places would never have leaked out if there had not been a "Whistle Blower". In the both instances the Whistle Blower had not been present during the massacres. In the Kimberleys it was the Reverend E. W Gribble, who learned of the killings through his native contacts. In

Vietnam it was because Private Ron Ridenhour's, who learned of the My Lei killings through friends who were there, became deeply troubled and decided to "spill the beans".

11. In both cases complaints by the Whistler Blowers initially fell on deaf ears. In Gribbles case his initial reports to the Australian Board of Missions and the Archbishop of Perth were ignored. It was only when he alerted the press that action developed. In Private Ridenhour's case his complaints did not get hearing until he compiled a four page report (12 months after the event) and sent copies to the Pentagon and members of US Congress. After the initial official enquiries there was a further attempts to cover up at the highest levels. In the Kimberleys, the Police Department and Government took no action on the report of Inspector Douglas which clearly indicated that a massacre had taken place. In Vietnam, Lieutenant General William Peers, who investigated the My Lei massacre was officially instructed not to refer to it a "massacre" or "war crime" but to refer to it as "a tragedy of major proportions", and he was further instructed not to make any mention of the raping and sodomising of young girls.

13. When the Governments of the day were forced by media coverage to take action, the subsequent trials were a farce. Captain Ernest Medina, Lieut Calley's immediate superior was hastily acquitted and Calley himself, although initially found guilty of 20 murders (after having been charged with 109), was sentenced to 20 years hard labour. On appeal this was reduced

to 10 years and on further appeal he was held in luxurious house arrest (with conjugal visits from a girl friend) and finally released on parole on President Nixon's orders. He did not spend one day in prison.

14. In both cases the perpetrators had strong public support, and both the people of the Kimberleys and American citizens subscribed substantial sums to enable those accused to have top level legal representation.
15. Both Whistle Blowers were treated as the "Bad Guys" by police and public in the Kimberleys , and by the Army and public in My Lei case. Both careers were wrecked by their whistle blowing actions.
16. In both apologies were never made, or any compensation, paid to families of the victims.

The two events seem to differ only in one significant respect. In the Kimberleys case no one involved could ever bring himself to write about the events of 1926. Lieutenant Calley had no such inhibitions. He wrote a book about the event, *The Battle Hymn of Lt. Calley* which sold 200,000 copies and made him a lot of money, some of which had to be spent on employing a secretary to answer all the letters of support he received at the time

All of which perhaps tells us more about the values of modern society than it does about people like Lieutenant Calley.

Bibliographical Notes

This volume lacks the tedious footnotes so beloved by Academia, but for those readers who would like to pursue further studies of some of the subjects covered, I have supplied below some bibliographical information on my major sources of information. These are arranged on a chapter by chapter basis and where I have considered a source of particular importance or worthy of special study I have indicated this with a notation "Recommended" in brackets.

CHAPTER 1 *The Boat People.*

When the Sky Fell Down, The Destruction of the Tribes of the Sydney Region 1788-1850's, Keith Willey. Collins, Sydney, 1979. (Recommended).

A Narrative of the Expedition To Botany Bay, Watkin Tench. London, 1789.

A Complete Account of the Settlement at Port Jackson, Watkin Tench. London 1793.

An Account of the English Colony in New South Wales – With Remarks on the Dispositions, Customs, Manners etc. of the Native Inhabitants of that Country, David Collins. From A H & A W Reedw Facsimile Edition 1975 (originally published London 1798).

Pemulway - The Rainbow Warrior, Professor Eric Willmot. Weldon, Sydney, 1987.

Creating a Nation: CHAPTER 1 -Birthplaces, Ann McGrath. McPhee Gribble, Melbourne, 1994. (Recommended).

The Destruction of Aboriginal Society - Aboriginal Policy and Practice -Vol I, C. D. Rowley. ANU Press, Canberra, 1970.

Archival material in the Mitchell Library, Sydney.

CHAPTER 2 *Hiccups of History.*

History of Dubbo (unpublished manuscript), James Jarvis (1949). Held by Dubbo City Council.

Dubbo Walkabout, Bill Hornadge. Review Publications, Dubbo 1977. Archival material held by Dubbo Museum & Historical Society.

CHAPTER 3 *The River Kings.*

Citizens, Eric Rolls. University Of Queensland Press, 1996.
River Boats, Ian Mudie. Rigby, Adelaide, 1961.
River Boat Days - On The Murray, Darling, Murrumbidgee, Peter Phillips. Lansdowne, 1972.
The River Trade - Wool & Steamers, Gwenda Painter. Turton & Armstrong with The Pioneer Settlement Press, 1987.
Echuca - A Centenary History, Susan Priestly. The Jacaranda Press, Brisbane, 1965.
Local Posts Of Australia, Bill Hornadge. Review Publications, Dubbo, 1982.
Hemisphere Magazine, July/August Issue 1983, Article By Morag Loh
Archival material held by the State Library of Victoria.
Archival Material held by the Echuca (Victoria) Museum.
Archival material held by the Wentworth (NSW) Museum.
The Australian Dictionary of Biography. Volume 5, 1850-1900.

CHAPTER 4 *The Vaucluse Snakes..*

The Story of Vaucluse House and Sir Henry Browne Hayes, Charles H Bertie. Vaucluse Parks Trust, Sydney, 1923. (Based on a paper read before the Australian Historical Society). (Recommended).
The Trial of Sir Henry Hayes, Knt for Forcibly and Feloniously taking away Miss Mary Pike, on the twenty second day of July 1797, before Mr Justice Day and a Most Respectable Jury, on the Thirteeth day of April 1801, taken down by an eminent shorthand writer.(Transcript of trial evidence) Published by James Haly, Cork, Ireland, 1801.
Home was Here, Mary Lang. Library of Australian History, Sydney, 1987. (Recommended).
Historical Records of New South Wales. Vol 5, Page 104.
Fragments of the Early History of Australia 1788-1812 (Pages 305-312), Compiled by John McMahon. W & J Barr, Melbourne 1913.
Australian Dictionary Of Biography 1788-1850. Vol 1,

CHAPTER 5 *Martial Law.*

Windradyne of the Wiradjuri - Martial Law at Bathurst 1824. Studies in Australian and Pacific History No 4, T Salisbury and P J Gresser; Edited by

Walter Stone. Wentworth Books, Sydney, 1971. (Recommended).
Memoirs of George Suttor - A Banksia Collector, Edited by George Mackaness. George Mackaness -Australian Historical Monograph series, Sydney,1948.
Blood on the Wattle, Bruce Elder. National Press, Sydney, 1988.
Archival material held in Mitchell Library, Sydney.

CHAPTER 6 *Henry's Mum.*

Louisa Lawson - Henry Lawson's Crusading Mother, Lorna Ollif. Rigby, Adelaide, 1978. (Recommended).
The First Voice of Australian Feminism - Excerpts from Louisa Lawson's *The Dawn* 1888-1895, Olive Lawson. Simon & Schuster, Sydney, 1990.
The Lonely Crossing - And Other Poems, By Louisa Lawson. The Dawn, Sydney, 1905.
Extended interview with Louisa Lawson published in The Bulletin October 24, 1896.

CHAPTER 7 *Remittance Men.*

A Splendid Type of the Genuine English Gentleman: Sir Frederick Pottinger, Bart, Article by P A Selth. Canberra Historical Journal, March 1974. (Recommended).
History of Dubbo, James Jarvis (1949). Unpublished manuscript by held by the Dubbo City Council. (Notes on Frederick Pottinger).
Archival material held on Isaac Robinson by Ric Robinson of Norfolk Island and collated by his wife (Colleen McCullough Robinson).
Research and notes supplied by Ruth Park (Mrs Darcy Niland) when she was resident on Norfolk Island and notes supplied by Tom Livingstone-Grimshaw, a resident of Norfolk Island.
Archival material held by the United States Department of State, Washington, DC.

CHAPTER 9 *A Yank Down Under.*

The Strange Career of Mr Hoover Under Two Flags, John Hamill. William Faro, New York, 1931 (Recommended).
Herbert Hoover - A Reminiscent Biography, By Will Irwin. Grossel & Dunlap, New York , 1928.
Those Were the Days, Arthur Reid. Barclay and Sharland, Perth, 1933.

Golden Destiny - The Centenary History of Kalgoorlie-Boulder and the Eastern Goldfields of Western Australia, Martyn and Audrey Webb. City of Kalgoorlie Boulder, 1993.
Camels And The Outback, H. M. Barker. Angus & Robertson Ltd in association with Sir Isaac Pitman & Sons Ltd, 1964.

CHAPTER 10 *The Mystery Axeman.*

The Secret Discovery Of Australia - Portuguese Ventures 200 years before Captain Cook, Kenneth Gordon Mclntyre. Souvenir Press, Menindie, SA, 1977.

CHAPTER 12 *A Piece of Dessicated Tissue.*

Rosenbach - The Life of One of the Greatest Book Collectors, Edwin Wolf and John Fleming. Weidenfeld and Nicholson, London 1960.

CHAPTER 13 *A Military Manoeuvre.*

Curtin's Cowboys - Australia's Secret Bush Commandos, Richard and Helen Walker. Allen & Unwin, Sydney, 1986. (Recommended).

CHAPTER 14 *Chidley's Answer.*

Confessions of William James Chidley. Unpublished manuscript in Mitchell Library, Sydney.
The Confessions of William James Chidley (Edited version of the above), S Mclnerney. Queensland University Press Brisbane, 1977.
Chidleys Answer to the Sex Problem, Bill Hornadge. Review Publications, Dubbo, 1983.
The Answer - Or the World as Joy -an Essay in Philosophy, W J Chidley (with an introduction by Profesor Francis Anderson). Sydney D Smith of 200 Castlereagh St, Sydney, 1915.
The Answer, William James Chidley. Self-published booklet in many varying editions, Melbourne and Sydney, circa 1908-1914.

CHAPTER 15 *The Unlucky Bullet.*

An Expert in the Service of the Soviet, Maurice Laserson. Ernest Benn Ltd, London, 1929.
From Russian Skies To The Southern Cross - Diary of an Intellectual, Maurice Laserson. Serialised in The Hebrew Standard, Sydney, 1950.

An Autobiography - and People I Have Met, David Laseron. Wilson & Son, Sydney 1904.
From Australia To The Dardenelles.-Being some Odd Pages from the Diary of Charles Francis Laseron, Sgt in the 13th Battalion AIF. John Sands Ltd, Sydney 1916.
South With Mawson, Charles Laseron. Angus & Robertson, Sydney, 1947.
The Face Of Australia, Charles Laseron. Angus & Robertson, Sydney 1953.
Ancient Australia, Charles Laseron. Angus & Robertson, Sydney, 1954.
Henry Parkes - A Biography, A. W. Martin. Melbourne University Press 1980.

CHAPTER 16 *Drama in Antarctica.*

The Home Of The Blizzard - The Story of the Australasian Antarctic Expedition of 1911-1914 -Vol I&II, Sir Douglas Mawson. Heinemann 1915. Facsimile edition by Wakefield Press, 1996.
Mawson's Antarctic Diaries, Edited by Fred Jacka and Eleanor Jacka. Allen & Unwin, Sydney, 1988.
South With Mawson, Charles Laseron. Angus & Robertson, Sydney, 1947.
Our Forgotten Polar Hero, Nikki Barrowclough. *Good Weekend Magazine*, June 29, 1996.

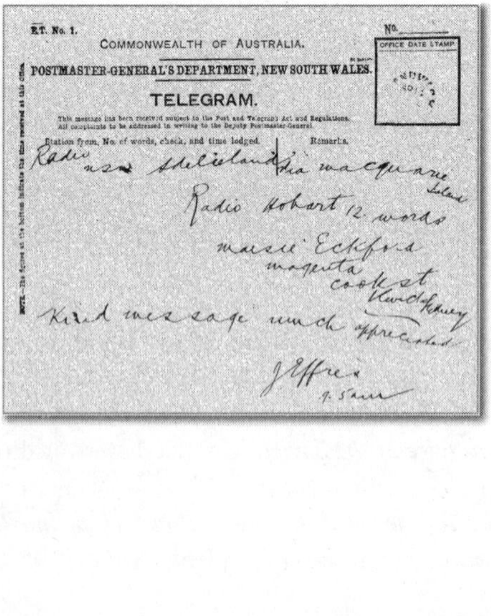
P.T. No. 1.
No.
COMMONWEALTH OF AUSTRALIA.
POSTMASTER-GENERAL'S DEPARTMENT, NEW SOUTH WALES.
OFFICE DATE STAMP
TELEGRAM.
This message has been received subject to the Post and Telegraph Act and Regulations.
All complaints to be addressed in writing to the Deputy Postmaster-General.
Station from, No. of words, check, and time lodged. | Remarks.
Radio
Radio Hobart 12 words
Eckford
magenta
cook st
Kind message much appreciated

CHAPTER 17 ***Our Politicians.***

I Remember, J. T. Lang (Chapter 40 : The Terrible History of T. J Ley). Invincible Press, Sydney, 1956.

New South Wales Parliamentary Records. Mitchell Library, Sydney.

Lady Rowena Log Book - April 25,1830 to June 1832, compiled by Captain Bourn Russell. Original held on loan in Mitchell Library, Sydney.

The Australian Encyclopaedia. Volume 5.

CHAPTER 18 ***The Beauteous Terrorist.***

The Beauteous Terrorist & Other Poems, by A Wanderer (Sir Henry Parkes). Self-published, Sydney, 1885.

CHAPTER 19 ***A Ticket in Tatts.***

The Romantic Career of Geo Adams, Hobart. Tattersalls Hobart, 1953.

The Australian Encyclopaedia. Vol I.

The Australian Philatelist. Winter 1989, Vol 2 No 2. Article: *Tattersalls and the Post Office.* By Richard Breckon.

The Australian Stamp Collector, Vol I No I, June 1991. Article *When the Post Office Banned Tattersalls.* By Richard Breckon.

The Luck of the Draw -a Centenary of Tattersall's Sweeps 1881-1981, Trevor Wilson. Wilson Publishing, Melbourne,1981.

CHAPTER 20 ***The Wentworths***

William Charles Wentworth of Vaucluse House, K. R Kramp MA. Self-published, Sydney, 1918.

Ratbags, Keith Dunstan. Golden Press, Sydney, 1979.

The Life And Times Of William Charles Wentworth - Patriot, Orator, Statesman, G. B. Barton. Serialised in The Australian Star, Sydney, 1898.

A Statistical Account of the British Settlements in Australasia - including the Colonies of New South Wales and Van Diemen's Land, Third edition, 2 volumes, W. C. Wentworth Esq, a native of New South Wales. Geo Whittaker, London, 1824.

Fragments of the Early History of Australia 1788-1812 (Land Grants to the Wentworths Page 397), Edited John McMahon. W & J Barr, Melbourne, 1913.

The Australian Dictionary Of Biography 1788-1850. Vol 2.

The Australian Encyclpaedia Vol 9.

CHAPTER 22 ***Australia's My Lei.***

Report of the Royal Commission of Inquiry Into Alleged Killing and Burning of Bodies of Aborigines in East Kimberley - and into Police Methods where effecting arrests, Commissioner G T Wood Esq. SM. Government Printer, Perth, 1927. (Recommended)
The Forrest River Massacres, Neville Green. Fremantle Arts Press, Perth, 1994. (Recommended).
Black Australians - A Survey of Native Policy in Western Australia 1829-1897, Paul Hasluck. Melbourne University Press, Melbourne, 1970.
Aboriginal Administration in Western Australia 1886-1905, Leslie R Marchant. The Australian Institute of Aboriginal Studies, Canberra, 1981.
Jandamarra - And the Bunuba Resistance, Howard Pedersen and Banjo Woorunmurra. Magabala Books, Broome 1995. (Recommended).
Field Notes on the Forrest River Mission 1927, Professor A P. Elkin.
Dark Deeds In A Sunny Land - Or Blacks and Whites in North-West Australia, The Rev J. B. Gribble. Originally published in 1905, and re-published in slightly amended form by the University of Western Australia Press, Perth 1987. (Recommended).
Forty Years With The Aborigines, The Rev E. R. Gribble. Angus & Robertson, Sydney, 1930.
A Despised Race, The Rev. E. R. Gribble. The Australian Board of Missions, Sydney, 1933.
Incident on Hill 192 - Casualties of War, Daniel Lang. Pan Books, London, 1970.
The Wound Re-opened. Time Magazine, April 12, 1971.
My Lei Story. The Australian Magazine -Article, June 3-4, 1989.